BECOMING A PERSON OF GOD

With Love
To

Thomas

Br. Stanly

7/1/2011

BECOMING A PERSON OF GOD

OF GOD

Understanding the process

SUNNY PHILIP

authorHOUSE®

AuthorHouse™
1663 Liberty Drive
Bloomington, IN 47403
www.authorhouse.com
Phone: 1-800-839-8640

First published by AuthorHouse   06/03/2011

ISBN: 978-1-4634-1649-2 (sc)
ISBN: 978-1-4634-1648-5 (dj)
ISBN: 978-1-4634-1647-8 (ebk)

Library of Congress Control Number: 2011909117

Printed in the United States of America

Any people depicted in stock imagery provided by Thinkstock are models, and such images are being used for illustrative purposes only.
Certain stock imagery © Thinkstock.

This book is printed on acid-free paper.

Because of the dynamic nature of the Internet, any web addresses or links contained in this book may have changed since publication and may no longer be valid. The views expressed in this work are solely those of the author and do not necessarily reflect the views of the publisher, and the publisher hereby disclaims any responsibility for them.

All Scripture quotations are taken from the New King James Version (NKJV) of the Holy Bible. Copyright 1988 Thomas Nelson, Inc. Used with permission.

CONTENTS

Acknowledgements

I gratefully acknowledge the help of the following people who made this book possible in this form: My wife Mercy and my three children, for putting up with me while I chase my convictions, Kimberly Kanhai, for transcribing the audio messages so that this process could start, Celin Jagessar, for proof reading the text and giving me suggestions and all the folks in our church Gateway World Christian center in New York, for pushing me to get this done. My special thanks to Wilfred Laurent, on whom myself and our church often call for graphic designs, for designing the cover. I am also grateful to Author House for their help in publishing this book.

Above all, all glory goes to my Heavenly Father, who inspired me through the life of David and taught me the lessons in this book that I have shared with others.

This book is dedicated to the memory of Late Pastor K.E. Abraham of India, who showed me through his life, what God can accomplish through a person fully dedicated to the call upon his life.

Preface

It has been my privilege to teach the Bible and preach from it around the globe for over twenty years now. Though I enjoy ministering in different parts of the world and among different people groups, my favorite pulpit is my local church, where I can systematically teach the word of God.

Among the thousands of sermons I have preached over these years, the most favorite seems to be the series I did on the life of David. In 2009, I preached on it a second time in a new church setting. It simply turned out to be a trip! Holy Spirit just took us on a trip that I did not plan. From the beginning, my heart was flooded with new thoughts inspired by Holy Spirit. People in my church came along for this trip and we had a good time!

By the time I finished the sermons, we had request for over four hundred CDs of these messages internally. So I knew people were really blessed by the messages God gave me. Since then our people have been encouraging me to turn those messages into a book.

This book is unusual in that most of the chapters are based on the transcription of the audio of the messages I gave live. So it does not neatly fall into a character study. I have not covered all the details about the life of David as you would in a character study. It is not a verse by verse study of any passages by any means. I have selected passages that can teach us spiritual lessons. So some chapters are based on a number of chapters in the Bible, whereas some other chapters are based on a couple of verses. Be ready to meet the preacher in me on many of these pages.

Thus it is part character study, part exhortation, part preaching and a little bit of everything, to be honest.

It is my prayer that the public in general will be equally blessed by reading this book. This book is a compilation of those messages.

Please take a moment to let me know, if these chapters inspire you as it did myself and my church members.

Dr. Sunny Philip

CHAPTER I

A God Who Prepares the Stage

As children, very few of us know where we will end up in life later. Some of us reach heights we never dreamt of. Some others dream big but crash their lives miserably. Some others live to see their lives reach heights and then plummet to abyss because of addictions or financial disasters.

In the life of a child of God, there is an extra dimension in play. That is the hand of God. Many times we fail to realize that there is a God who is interested in us personally and that he will set the stage for the people who trust in Him. That is what happened to David.

The story of David begins rather abruptly. While there is another king is on the throne, God sent Prophet Samuel to look for a new king in the house of Jesse. What Samuel was asked to do was an act of treason. By that afternoon's end, David was anointed to be the next king in Israel.

Why was God looking for a new king for Israel? Especially when God had asked the same prophet to anoint the reigning king? The fall of King Saul from grace is a solemn study.

Samuel had been serving the nation as a judge for forty years. He had a circuit around the nation. He would come to one of the four cities selected as listen to the complaints of the people, conduct sacrifices for people etc. Towards the end of his life, the people of Israel realized that the children of Samuel were not honest and godly persons like their father or any better than the children of Eli, whom he replaced as priest. So they came to him and asked for a king, like the other nations around them. They were not comfortable with the thought of Samuel's children becoming the next generation of leaders.

Samuel was naturally hurt and upset. But God told him that 'for they have not rejected you, but they have rejected Me, that I should not reign over them.' (1 Samuel 8:7). Israel was a theocracy until then.

Samuel told taught them that they could change the leadership without changing the system. If a king comes into power, he will definitely change the entire system they enjoyed for about five hundred years. But the people insisted.

The requirement from the people was simple. They needed a king "that we also may be like all the nations, and that our king may judge us and go out before us and fight our battles." 1 Sam. 8:20). God gave more than what they asked for.

King Saul hailed from the tribe of Benjamin and belonged to a wealthy family. He was a tall and handsome man. 'There was not a more handsome person than he among the children of Israel.' (1 Sam. 9:2)

Outwardly, Saul was a specimen they could proudly display in front of their neighbors. But inwardly, Saul was a different person. He was no leadership material!

As per the guidance of God, Samuel anointed Saul privately as king at his residence. Whomever God calls, He equips. As soon as he received the anointing, God gave him a new heart (10:9), signifying that a leader must think differently. Samuel prophesied other things over him. But none of that would manifest before he got a new heart.

In that chapter we can see three things in the life of a person God anoints to be a leader. First, He gives them a new heart and teaches them to think differently. Saul had already betrayed his thinking of unworthiness to Samuel in 1 Samuel 9:21. Humility is one thing. But being haunted by a feeling of unworthiness is not humility. God wanted Saul to think differently. Only then he could be an effective leader.

Secondly, Samuel told him that he would have new spiritual experiences. Saul would be prophesying with a group of prophet along the way, which would give him the confidence of God's presence in his life. Thirdly, Samuel told him that along the way, someone will give him a gift of loaves and to take it. It was a friendship gesture by total strangers. Saul was going to rule over people to whom he was a total stranger up to that point. When God calls someone into leadership, He also arranges a group of people who will accept that person as a leader. A leader is a person who has followers, not a person who has a title. The friendly gesture from total strangers was an indication to Saul that he would be accepted by Israel as their leader.

Then he called a meeting at Saul's house to make it official and to publicly present their new leader. But they could not find Saul! When he saw hundreds of people gathering at his house to coronate him, he went and hid himself in the hey. Samuel had to ask God for guidance to find out where Saul was. Thus, Saul was a reluctant king from the beginning. He was plagued with inferiority complex. He had not mastered the art of thinking like a leader yet.

The good thing is, anointing flows in the life of the least worthy people. How many people in ministry today will gladly confess to it—that they were not fit to be in the position they are today in the natural, but that the anointing has made all the difference in their lives!

As soon as Saul was proclaimed as the king in Israel, the Ammonites came up against them to challenge the new king under the leadership of their king Nahash. The new system was not even fully in place yet. In fact, when the challenge appeared, we find Saul still walking after the herd of his father. (11:5).

The new system had not sunk in the heart of Israelites either. They asked for a king 'to fight their battles.' But when Nahash challenged them, instead of asking their new king to lead them into war, they tried to enter into a peace deal with him. That is the way they survived for hundreds of years. Old ways are hard to break!

More incredible is the demand Nahash placed on them. He demanded their 'right eyes' to leave them alone. (11:2). A very strange demand indeed! Someone exclaimed once, "What was this king going to do with their eyes? Make a human eye soup?" Well, the eye represents vision. He was demanding them to give up on their vision.

It was a time of establishing order in Israel. Until then they were like the colonies of Europeans prior to USA became a republic. They lived, they survived. But now they were ready to be organized as a nation with central leadership under a king. Saul had even given them a preliminary constitution for the rule of monarchy. (1 Samuel 8:11-18).

The enemy came to stop the progress. He wanted to pluck out their eyes—destroy their vision. He wanted to leave them as a 'reproach,' a people who do not know how to forge their destiny with the leadership God has provided.

As soon as Saul heard this, the anointing in Saul began to function. After all, that is the purpose of the anointing. Many times people wonder what the big deal with anointing is. The value of anointing begins to manifest at the time of trials. "Then the Spirit of God came upon Saul when he heard this news, and his anger was greatly aroused." (1 Samuel 11:6). He sent the word out to come for battle and three hundred and thirty thousand people responded. The next day they went into battle and had a tremendous victory.

Challenges are not always bad. The enemy wanted to dishearten and scatter the people of God before the vision took root. But God turned that into a blessing. Saul was a new leader and not everyone had accepted him. Possibly the lack of self-confidence on the day of his coronation turned off some people. Some were already asking, "Shall Saul reign over us?" (11:12).

Thus the battle with Nahash became a ground for Saul to show the people that he has been equipped by God to handle the challenges through anointing, despite his natural shortcomings. His leadership was established that day and the nation turned a page. Samuel retired from his civil duties and Saul began to reign as king.

When God give us a new heart, it is important to move forward with it and not to fall back on our natural tendencies. Two years into his reign, we see self-doubts that Saul always had beginning to cause problems for him.

They were in battle with Philistines, which was a mighty established nation at a that time with iron chariots and a huge army. Israel had to fight them with crude weapons. So the people were in danger and they were distressed. (1 Samuel 13:6). They realized that they cannot have victory without the help of God and they wanted to a sacrifice for God under the leadership of Samuel, so that he can ask God for guidance in the battle.

The semi-retired Samuel took his time to get there. Saul found it hard to keep the people aligned with him until Samuel showed up. For seven days, it was total confusion in the Israelite camp. When a mighty enemy is lined up against you, when their screams of threats fall in your ears, when your own people are not sure how to handle it, the leader needs to show courage and confidence and the willingness to make the difficult decisions needed.

The followers always get their cue from the leader. Even small children read the emotions on the face of their parents and get their cues. If they see fear on the face of their parents, they will get afraid immediately. They know that their security is in the hands of their parents. The same goes for adults. People always want to get their cues from their leaders. Unfortunately, a leader lacking self-confidence will try to get his cues from his people.

Saul did the same. He got worried that the people will see the indecision in his life and will scatter. To save his face, he did something he should have never done. He offered to do the sacrifice himself. As soon as the sacrifice was over, here comes Samuel. When asked why he did something so foolish, Saul replied, "Therefore I felt compelled, and offered a burnt offering." (13:12). Under the pressure, I compromised!

What a tragic statement! But how true! Leadership is high pressure territory. But one cannot crack under pressure—especially when one claims to be anointed by God. That anointing is there to sustain you, to uphold you and to redeem you. What happened to Saul at that moment was reverting back to natural self—a life style of self-doubt and inferiority complex.

5

The event became the starting point of a downward spiral in his life. Even though he remained on the throne for another thirty eight years, things were different. God had showed tremendous mercy to an unworthy person. Saul read it wrong. His kingdom was being established. The people had accepted him as their leader. He just had to rise up to the occasion and tell them to wait for Samuel, since we are committed to keeping the commandments of the Lord. "But now your kingdom shall not continue. The LORD has sought for Himself a man after His own heart, and the LORD has commanded him to be commander over His people, because you have not kept what the LORD commanded you." (1 Samuel 13: 14).

The entire chapter is full of leadership mistakes. Just prior to attacking a garrison of powerful Philistines, Saul sent away all but four thousand soldiers to their tents. When the Philistines responded with thirty thousand chariots, Israel was in no shape to counter that. Saul's call for a sacrifice was a desperate attempt to cover up a leadership mistake. People saw right through it. And when the fiasco with the sacrifice unfolded, even the people who were with him began to scatter. You cannot hold the people together with gimmicks. In the end, Saul had six hundred people with him. (1 Samuel 13:15).

It is a verdict from the people. When they had confidence in him, thirty eight thousand people came out to join him in battle. Now it is down to six hundred. Look what happens if we do not handle the leadership opportunities God give us wisely.

We see the beginning of a downward spiral here. The second stage was the rash decision he made in 1 Samuel 14. The battle with Philistines is dragging on. Israel was in a dire situation. "Now there was no blacksmith to be found throughout all the land of Israel, for the Philistines said, "Lest the Hebrews make swords or spears."" (1 Samuel 13:19). They were forced to go to the Philistines even to sharpen their ploughshares.

In that situation, Saul's son Jonathan decided to trust in God and do some exploits. He had concluded that 'For nothing restrains the LORD from saving by many or by few.' (14:6). Later in that battle, as God was giving them victory, King Saul made a rash proclamation.

"And the men of Israel were distressed that day, for Saul had placed the people under oath, saying, "Cursed [is] the man who eats [any] food until evening, before I have taken vengeance on my enemies." So none of the people tasted food." (1 Samuel 14:24)

The leader was asking his people to fight a battle on empty stomach! Jonathan who was with another garrison did not know about this and ate a honey comb. When his father found out about it, he almost killed his own son for not keeping the oath. The people of Israel had to rise up against the King to protect Jonathan.

The anointing was still at work in Saul. God will use us for the cause we are called for, despite our shortcomings. "So Saul established his sovereignty over Israel, and fought against all his enemies on every side, against Moab, against the people of Ammon, against Edom, against the kings of Zobah, and against the Philistines. Wherever he turned, he harassed them."(1 Samuel 14:47).

The next step in the downward spiral happened in 1 Samuel 15. Saul had a tendency to take liberty with things. As the son of a wealthy family, he probably did not have to follow rules when he was a young man. As an adult, Saul definitely had an issue in that area. In 1 Samuel 13, he took liberty and offered the sacrifice which led to a warning from the Lord that he will take the kingdom away from Saul and his family. But in chapter 15, we see Saul taking liberties again.

He was at war with Amalekites. He had a specific mission given to utterly destroy them, since that was prophesied a long time ago by Moses. Saul was the person to do it. He won the war. But did not carry out the mission faithfully. "But Saul and the people spared Agag and the best of the sheep, the oxen, the fatlings, the lambs, and all [that was] good, and were unwilling to utterly destroy them. But everything despised and worthless, that they utterly destroyed." (1 Samuel 15:9).

This new incident caused God to announce his disappointment publicly through Samuel. Yet, when Saul and Samuel met, Saul proclaimed, "I have performed the commandment of the LORD." (15:13). Samuel's reply was very poignant. "What then is this bleating of the sheep in my ears, and the lowing of the oxen which I hear?" Saul did not even realize that he had compromised! Saul kept on defending himself. Finally Samuel said, "Has the LORD as great delight in burnt offerings and sacrifices, as in obeying the voice of the LORD? Behold, to obey is better than sacrifice, and to heed than the fat of rams. For rebellion is as the sin of witchcraft, and stubbornness is as iniquity and idolatry. Because you have rejected the word of the LORD, He also has rejected you from being king." (1 Samuel 15:22,23).

The next turning point came when Saul became jealous of David. It was another battle with the Philistines. This time they came not with iron chariots, but with a giant. The enemy made it really personal. In between God had sent Samuel to the house of Jesse in Bethlehem to find the next king in Israel. (We have dedicated the next chapter for that incident).

When David had victory over Goliath and the young ladies in Israel were singing his praises, Saul became very jealous. He began to realize that he may end up giving his kingdom to this young man. By now, he had used to being royalty and wanted the kingship to remain in his family. The man who was hiding from kingship does not want to give it up now. In his mind he was all worked up. It became an obsession for him. A distressing spirit from the Lord came upon David (18:10). His only comfort was when David would take the harp and play. It would drive him madder that the man he wants to kill is the man ministering to him. He tried to kill David a number of times.

Even after David was driven out of the palace, Saul was not satisfied. He chased him all over the country to catch and kill him. A man in whom Holy Spirit flowed freely at one time is now totally controlled by a murderous spirit. That spirit never left him until he killed himself on the mountains of Gilboa.

The last turning point in his life was when Saul started looking for a medium. Early in his rule, he had killed all the witches as a part of cleansing the land. In those days, he used to hear from the Lord regularly through Samuel. But Samuel refused to see him after the fiasco with Amalekites. The Bible says that God 'the LORD did not answer him, either by dreams or by Urim or by the prophets. (1 Samuel 28:6). So he became desperate and the same king who killed the witches (28:9) started looking for one. She found one in Endor and used her to consult to the spirit of Samuel. The sad answer he got was 'why bother me if God has left you?' Frustrated Saul had his last meal in the house of that medium and the next day he killed himself.

The story of Saul is that of a tragic leader who did not know how to use the grace that was showed to him. He wasted it and died a total failure. A line from the song David wrote to commemorate the life of Saul says it all: "O mountains of Gilboa, Let there be no dew nor rain upon you, nor fields of offerings. For the shield of the mighty is cast away there! The shield of Saul, not anointed with oil." (2 Samuel 1:21). What led the downward spiral in the life of Saul was not taking care of the anointing he received.

But in the midst of this dark chapter entered David as a bright star of hope, anointed by God to lead his people and establish the kingdom of ancient Israel to its glorious zenith.

CHAPTER II

Understanding God's Choice

In the last chapter we saw the predicament in which Israel was after Saul was established as king. He did not provide right leadership for the nation. His rash decisions many times ended up in disaster. Samuel stopped meeting with him to give him counsel. God declared that He regretted making Saul the king. God in Saul gave the Israelites a king who looked good in the sight of the people. History proved that he was not the right choice for the king. So God told Samuel to go the house of Jesse, where he has found a 'man after His own heart,' a king who would rule the way God wanted to rule.

Samuel was not ready for that task. After all, he was the one who anointed Saul as the king. Who want to go public after anointing someone as king and acknowledge that he made a mistake? Samuel had a reputation as a 'true prophet of the Lord' frond Dan to Beersheba. (1 Samuel 3:20). How could he admit that he made a mistake? What will happen to his prophetic ministry?

There was another issue Samuel had to confront. To anoint another persona s king while a king is still ruling on the throne is treason. The reigning king could, if he wanted to, kill Samuel for doing it. Plus, in this case, Samuel is the one who gave them the constitution for monarchy and asked people to follow that. Now he was being asked by God to violate the law that he helped to institute. It was not an easy task for Samuel.

God wanted to use Samuel to bring an end to the time period in the history of Israel when judges ruled the land and the nation became a monarchy. Both Samuel and the people had erred in this matter. When Samuel, the true prophet, appointed his unruly children as judges over Israel, he was trying to slip in the monarchy into his own household. That was not God's choice. When people asked for a king, in response to the move Samuel made, it was also not in line with the plan of God. Moses had a long time told them that one day they would have kings. But no one is waiting for God's timing or God's person. Saul was a temporary fix until God's choice was revealed.

The Bible says Samuel mourned for Saul. God asked him one day, "How long will you mourn for Saul, seeing I have rejected him from reigning over Israel?" Samuel did not want to go through another anointing. He just wanted Saul to understand his mistakes and get right with God. But it was becoming more and more clear that Saul's life was going in a different direction and he was in a downward spiral.

Ultimately, if you are a servant of God chosen to do something, you end up doing it. So God commanded Samuel, "Fill your horn with oil, and go; I am sending you to Jesse the Bethlehemite. For I have provided Myself a king among his sons." So Samuel went to Bethlehem.

He had to do this wisely. So he sent word that he was coming over for a sacrifice. It was a sacrifice and a dinner, like in a thanksgiving sacrifice. A small portion of the animal was offered as sacrifice and the rest of the meat was used for a communal meal. When Samuel got there, he made his plans known to Jesse and asked him to bring his sons. As soon as he saw the first born, Eliab, he declared, "Surely the LORD's anointed [is] before Him!" (1 Samuel 16:6). He was big and strong like Saul and Samuel knew that people would accept him as a replacement for Saul. He was a career military man and been in a few battles already. This could be the person!

When God said no to Eliab, Samuel was kind of surprised. But when he looked at the next son, he was just as good looking and strong as Eliab. But God said no to him also. In fact God said no to every single person present there.

Finally God said, "For the LORD does not see as man sees; for man looks at the outward appearance, but the LORD looks at the heart." (16:7). What did that mean? Samuel was thinking in terms of a replacement for Saul, who people had no problem accepting. So he wanted someone with the looks and physical structure of Saul. But there is no correlation between anointing and physical stature. God said, No, this is not another experiment. I told you before I sent you to the house of Jesse that My goal is reveal the person after My own heart. So keep looking until you find that person." Samuel looked around. There were no other sons around.

So finally he asked, "Are all the young men here?" Only then Jesse mentioned anything about David. "Then he said, There remains yet the youngest, and there he is, keeping the sheep." (16:11). Samuel asked for him to be brought from the pasture.

It was getting sticky for Samuel too. He wanted to finish off the project before word got around. But now he had to wait for David to come from the wilderness.

There are many different interpretations about why Jesse acted that way. Some people say, David was possibly born from another woman or even a concubine of Jesse. It is highly unusual that the older boys are home and the youngest was sent out to the forest to take care of the sheep! I tend to think that Jesse also was thinking like Samuel. If someone from that family was going to replace Saul, that person must have the physique and stature of Saul. David was just a 'ruddy' young kid with bright eyes and how was he going to replace Saul?

Look at this statement about Saul: 'And he had a choice and handsome son whose name was Saul. There was not a more handsome person than he among the children of Israel. From his shoulders upward he was taller than any of the people.' (1 Samuel 9:2) Compare it with this statement about David: 'Now he was ruddy, with bright eyes, and good-looking.' (1 Samuel 16:2)

As soon as David showed up, God told Samuel, "Arise, anoint him; for this is the one!" Samuel anointed David as the next king, as God asked him.

How grateful we should be that God is specific in His calling! No one can take your place in the kingdom of God. Whatever God want to accomplish through you will be accomplished only through you. Others may want your anointing, but it is reserved for you. Others may want your ministry, but it is reserved for you. The anointing will not flow until you are on the scene. God will send someone looking for you when you least expect it or looking for it. No wonder David wrote later, "O LORD, You are the **portion** of my inheritance and my cup; You maintain my lot." (Psalms 16:5). Any blessing that is yours will remain until get there. No one will touch your future, your promotion, and your rewards. God will maintain your lot.

God is waiting for some of you like He waited for David. The horn has been filled with oil for a while. But you are not ready yet. God is still waiting for you to arrive. Do not keep Him waiting forever.

The first principle we learn from this is that God's standards are different from ours and that God will not compromise when He chooses someone to accomplish His purpose. His choice may surprise us. But it was already decreed in heaven.

The second principle is that it involves a person's heart. There are similarities between the anointing of Saul and David. Both of them were not looking for it. Both were chosen by God and anointed by the same prophet and using the same horn. Both did not consider themselves worthy of the honor. But there is a glaring difference. Saul never grew into the anointing. He was always uncomfortable with the fact that God chose him. Whereas, David immediately accepted it and started growing into God's purpose.

This teaches us that even God cannot use everyone. One must be willing to work with God if he or she is to accomplish His purposes. One needs to accept the call and surrender. Many people were reluctant to accept the call initially—Moses, Gideon, Jeremiah etc. are examples in the Bible. But once they realized their call, they could not be shaken. They stayed on course even when they had to pay a huge price. Unfortunately, we cannot say the same thing about Saul. They may stumble, struggle and go through issues. But they will never reject the call upon their lives. They will never turn around and ask, "God, why did you choose me?" David never did that. Jeremiah never did that. Paul never did that. Are you comfortable in your calling?

God will usually train by using you for small things, where you can see that God has called you and you personally get an idea about where you may excel in God's kingdom. The magnitude of the job is not important since God is more interested in the heart with which you do your job. Big stages will come later, if you are faithful in little things.

Joyce Mayer has talked many times about her early days in ministry when she was just doing Bible studies in her living room. She was struggling with a smoking habit initially. She would smoke a cigarette alone and then come out and take a Bible class. Part of it was due to ignorance. Even in those days she was sure that God had called her to teach the Bible and there was no quitting. So she made the changes necessary in her lifestyle. Look where she is today.

What was so special about David's heart anyway? Alan Redpath in his book on David tells us that Psalm 23 shows what kind of a heart David had. According to him, Psalm 23 shows a believing heart (v.1), a meditating heart (v.2), a heart set on righteousness (v.3) and a heart of gratitude (v.5). [1]

The historical details are given to us in the books of 1 Samuel, 2 Samuel and 1 Chronicles. Chronicles were based on court diaries written by a paid employee of the king on the throne. That is why the accounts in Chronicles are a litter more rosy. In the case of David, we have another source—the Psalms he wrote. It is in the Psalms that he gives us a window to peer into his heart. We see him pouring out his feelings of betrayal, frustrations and deep dependence on God in the pages of Psalms. He tells us exactly how he felt when people gave upon him, when his own son rose up against him, when the cities where sought refuge betrayed him. We see that David was just like us in many respects, but always dependent on God and refusing to give upon himself or his god. We see a pious man who meditated on God day and night, who prayed up to seven times a day.

The third principle is that God will always publicly recognize whom he has chosen. David was anointed 'in the midst of his brothers.' (1 Samuel 16:13). When there was a question about the spiritual authority of Aaron, God allowed his dry rod to bloom, flower and bear fruits within twenty four hours in front of the entire camp of Israel. (Numbers 17:8).

When Paul was called by God at the city gate of Damascus, it was made clear that he was being called a witness of the gospel before Israel, gentiles and princes. "He is a chosen vessel of Mine to bear My name before Gentiles, kings, and the children of Israel." (Acts 9:15). For a while, he was just a Bible teacher in a local church. People had a tough time accepting Paul even in that capacity. But when the time came, the Holy Spirit publicly asked the church to separate him for the ministry for which he was called. (Acts 13:2).

God will do the same for everyone called by Him today. Sometimes there is a gap of time between your call and your public recognition. Do not dwell on it. Be faithful in what God has called you to do. When the time comes, god will set the stage for you.

David was making songs and singing them in the wilderness using crude instruments for years. No one paid attention to it. But look at your Bible. More than half of the Psalms are written by David. No one who knew David as a child tinkering with instruments thought it was the beginning of such a great life. It may be the same with you. There may be a great writer, a great musician or a great preacher waiting to be discovered in you.

One of thought that will come to us is this. If God rejected Saul, how come He did not reject David? If Saul did stupid things, David did stupider things. Saul tries to kill his own son to keep an oath. David actually caused the death of one of his faithful soldiers to keep a secret. David had many failures later in his life, which we will look at in future chapters. Did God make a mistake in selecting David?

Once again the heart made all the difference. Becoming a person after god's own heart is a process, not an overnight deal.

When we accept the call and realize we are in this for long haul and stay on course God will guide us and bring us back. Even when we are unfaithful, He will remain faithful. (1 John 1:9).

God's promise all along was if your heart is in the right place, I can work with you. David's heart was always in the right place. If he made a mistake, he would acknowledge it and cry in the presence for God asking for restoration. 'Restore unto me the joy of my salvation,' he would cry. He would always walk humbly before the Lord. He would seek to bring glory to God. He would always honor God.

God processed the heart of David until he became a man after God's own heart. Despite the struggles in his life, he died as a noble king, highly established and respected in that generation. But the Bible's testimony is different: "For David, after he had served **his** own **generation** by the will of God, fell asleep, was buried with **his** fathers." (Acts 13:36). It was not about David, but what God wanted to accomplish through him.

Chapter III

Lessons From a Battle

There is probably no one who has not heard the story of David and Goliath. So our goal in this chapter is not to reiterate the story, but to learn some spiritual lessons from this story.

Philistines and Israel had wars always between them. The Philistines used to oppress the Israelites for generations and the Israelites used to give them a portion of their harvest. When Saul became the king, he had victory over them already. But now the Philistines have come back. Last time they came with iron chariots. But this they came with a giant. The giant made himself a spokesperson for the Philistines and he challenged the Israelites to find someone to represent them. "Why have you come out to line up for battle? [Am] I not a Philistine and you the servants of Saul? Choose a man for yourselves, and let him come down to me." He shouted, "If he is able to fight with me and kill me, then we will be your servants. But if I prevail against him and kill him, then you shall be our servants and serve us." (1 Samuel 17: 8, 9). "Give me a man!" he screamed.

But the Israelites did not have a man. We are surprised that King Saul who was anointed by God did not go forward to meet the challenge. Things had turned for the worse since a previous battle with Amalekites, where he 'feared the people' and offered the sacrifice by himself. That day God left him. The Bible says that Samuel did not see Saul after that. (1 Samuel 15:35). So there is no divine guidance coming into his life. He is struggling to hold on to his throne somehow.

One should wonder why Jonathan did not show courage to face the challenge after the heroics in a previous battle with Philistines. He single handedly turned the tide in Israel's favor because of his conviction that "nothing restrains the LORD from saving by many or by few." (1 Samuel 14:6). He and his armor bearer started a slaughter of the enemies which encouraged the rest of the camp to come out of their hiding places and pursue the Philistines. That day God gave a resounding victory for Israel.

If Jonathan had gone forward this time, the people would have followed him. But he did not! Why? It cannot be that Jonathan lost the faith in God after witnessing how God honored him for taking a stand trusting in Him. It must be the after effects of that battle that rattled him.

King Saul had made another rash decision that day and declared that if anyone ate during that day, he would be put to death. Without knowing that decree, when Jonathan came across wild honey, he ate some of it. At the end of the war, it became a big issue. Instead of rejoicing in the victory God gave, there was a casting the lot to find out who violated the oath the king made and Jonathan was put on the spot light. The king was ready to kill his son whom God used to give them victory. But the community rose up against that defended Jonathan. The whole incident should have shaken him.

Now when Goliath was challenging them, Jonathan just stayed on the sidelines. Like our young people, he just exclaimed, 'whatever!'

The battle dry went on forty days. One can assume that within the camp of Philistines, they were wondering what is wrong with Goliath. Could he not see how scattered and scared the camp of Israel is? Could he not see that despite his cry day in and day out, no one showing up to confront him? Why did he not just attack them and finish them off? What is he waiting for?

What was he waiting for? When you ponder that question, you realize how true is the statement in Daniel that 'the Most

High rules in the kingdom of men!' (Daniel 4:17). We realize that God truly is in control of history.

Despite the bickering in the Philistine camp to finish off the Israel and go home, the champion continued his ego trip, challenging the Israelites, "Give me a man that I may fight with him." It went on for forty mornings and evenings, so that the word spread throughout the land about this unusual siege.

There were three soldiers in Saul's army who could have come forward and proved their worth that day. They were the older sons of Jesse. 'The three oldest sons of Jesse had gone to follow Saul to the battle. The names of his three sons who went to the battle [were] Eliab the firstborn, next to him Abinadab, and the third Shammah.' (1 Samuel 17:13). They were career military men and were really upset that Samuel did not anoint any of them to be the next king in Israel. This was their opportunity to prove to the world that Samuel was wrong in anointing their baby brother bypassing them. This was their chance to show their mettle and prove to the nation that they were ready to lead the nation.

The field was wide open for anyone. In fact the king had sweetened the deal. "The man who kills him the king will enrich with great riches, will give him his daughter, and give his father's house exemption from taxes in Israel." (1 Samuel 17:25). Yet, none of these three soldier sons of Jesse came forward to give it a try. It was proof from their part that God did not make a mistake.

After a few weeks, Jesse realized that the army rations would have run out by now. He was concerned about his sons and asked David to take a platter of cheese and some other foods to his brothers and their captain. David did not expect to be involved in the battle.

Little did he know that God was preparing a grand stand for choice to be shown to the whole nation. When David arrived at the camp, it was right on cue for Goliath to go on one of his tirades. "I defy the God of Israel," he shouted. It is only natural that he was becoming bolder and bolder seeing no one was coming forward to accept his challenge. Goliath knew that the victory for Israel depended on their God, since they did not have iron chariots or even enough swords or spears. The Philistines had already made sure of that. (1 Samuel 13:19, 20).

As soon as David heard Goliath defying his God, the anointing within began to rise up and there was a holy anger within him. He asked, "Who is this uncircumcised Philistine, that he should defy the armies of the living God?" 'Why are you all standing around od hiding behind the stones, when this guy is insulting you and your God?'

David ran into a group of men day dreaming. It is from them that he learned about the promises of Saul. They were probably saying among themselves, "Man, I wish I could take this guy out. Imagine becoming the son in law of the king. Imagine our properties becoming tax exempt forever. Imagine marrying beautiful Michal. How nice will be that!" Despite drooling over the prospects, they did not have the courage or confidence to lead that charge. David asked them, "What did you say? What will be given to the man who takes out this guy?" Not that he was thinking about marriage at that time, being just a teenager. He could not understand how a group of men could stand around and listen to the insult from another man for forty days without doing anything about it. They needed a new leader who would inspire them.

Just the tone of voice of David enough to get a new conversation going in the camp of Israel. Eventually it reached the ears of his older brothers and even the king.

Despite the show of confidence, not everyone took David seriously. In fact, we four obstacles David had to overcome before doing what God was preparing him to do. First, his father did not take him seriously. In the last chapter we saw how his father forgets all about him when Samuel came as an honored guest for dinner in his house. Everyone else was there. But young David was left in the field. It took a divine intervention to bring David to the home and to be anointed. Secondly, his siblings did not take him seriously. For them, it was the 'pride and insolence of the heart' of David that was being manifested and causing a burr in the camp, not the anointing upon him. (1 Samuel 17:28). 'How come you are not with the sheep?' 'How come you are not where we want you to be? How come you dare to go beyond us?'—A lot of questions generally posed by people who want to tie you down to the place they have destined for you.

What surprises me is that it was in front of them that God had anointed David to be the next king in Israel. Their response in the camp shows that they did not take it seriously. 'Ya, right! Our baby brother is going to be the next king in Israel?' I wonder what was the interpretation they gave to the public about Samuel's visit.

Thirdly, when the news reached Saul and David was summoned to his presence, he did not take him seriously. And Saul said to David, "You are not able to go against this Philistine to fight with him; for you are a youth, and he a man of war from his youth." (1 Samuel 17:33). Elsewhere the Bible tells us that 'David was ruddy in his face' which makes us think that he did not have a beard and therefore he was nothing but a teenager. What could he do against a giant?

Finally, when David was running up the hill later to confront the enemy, Goliath took one lone look at this person who finally showed up to confront him and despised him. So the Philistine said to David, "Am I a dog that you come to me with sticks?" What can you do to a giant like me?

Then, how did David get the chance to confront the giant? Because of his testimonies! He shared his experiences after the anointing fell on him to Saul.

"But David said to Saul, "Your servant used to keep his father's sheep, and when a lion or a bear came and took a lamb out of the flock, I went out after it and struck it, and delivered [the lamb] from its mouth; and when it arose against me, I caught [it] by its beard, and struck and killed it. Your servant has killed both lion and bear; and this uncircumcised Philistine will be like one of them, seeing he has defied the armies of the living God."" (1 Samuel 17:34-36).

These were private battles in his life. My conviction is that the goal of the lion and bear was not really the lamb. They were instruments used by Satan to finish off David before the world could ever see what he would become because of the anointing. That was the formative time period in David's life—fighting unexpected battles alone and wondering why he was going through all of that.

The formative years of our lives are extremely important. Who we are today is the sum total of where we have been in the past. How he responded to each situation in our life will influence where we end up in life. (How God forgives our failures and give us a second chance is a different story. That will come up later in our discussions).

God was providing isolated opportunities for David to see for himself how powerful the anointing on his life was. In the natural, a teenager cannot do what David did with the lion or a bear. It was certainly not his natural strength. The anointing provides 'the surpassing greatness of the power of God in our earthen vessels.' (2 Corinthians 4:7). David experienced that and it gave him a tremendous confidence to face any challenges that any come against him. What is our testimony? What have we done with the anointing upon our lives?

Once Saul heard the testimony, he changed his mind and blessed David. He gave him his military dress and sword. David tried to walk in it but could not. When God is setting you up to do great things, you do not need to walk in another person's anointing. It is true that Elisha asked for a double portion of Elijah's anointing. He did not ask to walk in Elijah's anointing. When we study Elisha's life, we see that his ministry was very different from that of Elijah. It is also true that God promised to send someone with the spirit of Elijah. (Malachi 4:6). That was for a generation for that needed the Elijah type of ministry again.

David knew that he did not kill the lion and the bear with a sword. His protection was not in military armor. So he decided to trust completely in God and charges up the hill to confront the enemy.

It looks like Goliath did not expect a little boy to come against him. He was ready for a military person in military garbs and having a sword or a spear in his hand. This is something I share with the young people. The enemy has seen the older generation in battle already. He knows their *modus operand*. Whereas, he has no clue the new generation with a fresh anointing will do the battle. That gives them a tremendous advantage. They are stealth until their victory become history.

Despite despising him, when Goliath looked at the face of David and listened to his confident words, he was startled. He immediately started cursing David in the name of his gods. I believe he was calling on his gods for back up just in case. David realized the spiritual dimension of the battle right away.

> "Then David said to the Philistine, "You come to me with a sword, with a spear, and with a javelin. But I come to you in the name of the LORD of hosts, the God of the armies of Israel, whom you have defied. This day the LORD will deliver you into my hand, and I will strike you and take your head from you. And this day I will give the carcasses of the camp of the Philistines to the birds of the air and the wild beasts of the earth, that all the earth may know that there is a God in Israel."" (1 Samuel 17: 45, 46).

He considered himself to be fighting this battle on behalf of the God of Israel. The giant also looked at himself as a person with the blessings of his gods to destroy Israel. Oh, only we could realize the spiritual dimensions of the battles we wage!

With a sling and a stone, David overcame the enemy who came with a bronze helmet on his head, armed with a coat of mail, bronze armor on his legs and a bronze javelin between his shoulders and a shield-bearer who went before him. How true was David's assessment! All he needed was the backup of the God of Israel. Weapons of our warfare are not carnal. (2 Corinthians 10:4).

What is the battle in your life today? Who is the giant defying you and threatening you? Have you experienced the faithfulness of God in your life? Can you build up your faith based on your previous experiences? The same God who helped you in the past is able to give you victory in your bigger battles today. Trust in Him and dare to confront the enemy. The victory belongs to you.

Chapter IV

Anatomy of a True Friendship

When we study the Bible we know that David was not a perfect person. He was a person with many failures yet God called him as a man after His own heart. So we know that there was a process, there was a evolution in his life where God took him from where he was in the natural to a level where he became what God wanted him to be. We are learning lessons from David's life so that we can also be a person—a man or a woman of after God's own heart.

In this chapter we take a look at a very unique friendship that David had with another young man named Jonathan. Let us start at 2 Samuel 1:26-27. This is a song that David wrote at the death of Jonathan commemorating his memory and trying desperately to keep his memory alive. This is what David said, "I am restless for you my brother Jonathan. You have been very pleasant to me. Your love to me was wonderful, surpassing the love of women." I want to stop there for a second because we live in a very wicked generation when you see the phrase "your love was better than the love of women" at least some people may get crazy ideas in their mind. So what kind of a relationship did David and Jonathan have? I have heard people twisting this in certain circles. So let us address it. When people think the friendship between David and Jonathan was anything but normal, it is because of the ignorance of the Eastern culture.

In the Eastern culture it is very common even to this day for men to have a very close bond and spend hours together. You can see that even among the young men from Eastern cultures in our church in New York. It is part of that Eastern culture. In our generation, unfortunately, everything becomes sexualized. So as soon as you see the phrase (even in the Bible), "Your love is every better than the love of women" people say ah ha. That is a mistake and a tragedy.

In verse 27 it says, "How the mighty have fallen and the weapons of war perished". Now Jonathan was the son of the previous King in Israel called King Saul. We have covered King Saul in the past and we will come back to Saul in the future because the life of King Saul and David were intertwined for a very long time. The uniqueness of this friendship is based on one fact, Jonathan was supposed to the next King. If you are the King's son, you are the next King. If you are the prince you are heir apparent and David is somebody that God is raising up to take the place of this heir apparent, the next King in line. So if you see somebody rising up to take your place, you do not become friends with them! Would you?

If you know that at your workplace it is happening in this generation because of the exportation of jobs to other nations or outsourcing. I know that this happened to somebody in our own church. You are sent to another country to train some people in that country. Initially you feel very happy that the company is sending you at the company's expense to go to India or China or wherever this outsourcing is taking place. They put you in nice hotel, take care of all of your expenses and you are getting a free trip to India or China so you are very happy. You go and pour your heart out wanting to be a good employee. So you train them very well only to come back and find out a week later that you were training them to take your job. How many of you know what I am talking about? It is happening to all corporations across this land. Many people have been burned by this process of outsourcing.

Yet here is David and Jonathan facing a similar situation. Not outsourcing, but God is raising David to take the kingdom away from Jonathan and Jonathan becomes his best friend. That does not happen in human history. If you see somebody rising up to take your place you would consider him as an enemy, right? You watch over him and in order to you make sure it does not happen, you start playing politics or whatever else you need to do to protect your position. But Jonathan did not do any of that. Instead he became the closest friend David ever had in his life. That is why this friendship is very unique. Let us find out why and how that happened.

The first encounter between these two people happens in 1 Samuel 18. While I was preparing this a couple of questions came to my mind. How come Saul did not confront the Goliath and I also asked you how come Jonathan did not confront Goliath? We know that Jonathan was an anointed young man and a man who already had won victory. He had full confidence in God but nonetheless Jonathan did not go and confront Goliath. Instead waited so that David could come on the stage. So one of the questions that we need to ask and analyze is why did Jonathan not go and confront Goliath even when he knew he had the confidence, he had the anointing, he had faith in God. What we see is somebody caught up in a system.

Jonathan was a young man who was caught up in a system that belonged to his father. His father was still sitting on the throne and he was the anointed crowned King. Jonathan was a very obedient son who never stood against his father. When we looked at the life of King Saul earlier, we saw folly after folly that was happening in this father's life and how he was slowly going away from God and the presence of God was departing. The anointing had departed, the peace had departed and we see that even in the midst of all of that Jonathan still remained a perfect son to a messed up father. There is a beautiful message about family relationship there.

In 1 Samuel 15, Jonathan went forward in another battle and had victory and came back and father got very angry because the father had a problem—he was plagued with an inferiority complex. So even though he was not able to do anything, anytime somebody else went forward to do something it affected him. He would get angry even if it is his own son, But Jonathan at the same time wanted to respect his father. How many of you get trapped in that kind of family situations? Sometimes that happens in husband and wife relationship. The wife may be a very smart, capable young lady (I know a number of young ladies like that) and the husband looks at them as a threat instead of enjoying their success and praising God and thanking Him for giving them a smart woman. They get threatened by the abilities of their wives. Sometimes you get trapped in family situations like that.

Unfortunately, that is where Jonathan was. He is the son of the king and supposed to be the next King. Every time he gets another victory he gets more popular with the people. So that is what the King wants, right? Any king will want his son to be more popular with the people so that by the time he is ready to hand over the throne to his son, the people are ready to receive him. That would be the natural turn of events. But this King, because of the inferiority complex that he was plagued with, did not look at the situation that way. Anyone who rose up became a threat to him.

We see this in some organizations also. Sometimes wonderful people with tremendous talents and qualities are caught up in dead end jobs because the people above them make sure that they will never go up, never get the promotion, never get an opportunity to show what they can really do. So these are all real life situations. We are not just reiterating a story that is three thousand years old. We are learning lessons that are practical and applicable in today in our lives.

So Jonathan knew he could not go and confront Goliath, even though he was ready to go and had the faith that God would give him victory. He did not want another family problem. So he stayed back probably was praying, "Lord send somebody, send somebody." You know we also do the same when God ask us to do things. Instead of taking that step of faith, we sit back and pray," Lord send somebody, Lord send somebody." It may be we are ashamed of the way we lived in the past, may be because of the baggage we think we are carrying or other people think we are carrying, that we never take that step forward. God will send somebody to do the task.

God did send somebody in Jonathan's place and David came on the scene and David had this tremendous victory. When we look at chapter 18, we see that immediately Jonathan connected with David. "Now when he finished speaking to Saul the soul of Jonathan was knit to the soul of David. Jonathan loved him as his own soul." (18:1). What is happening here? When David came on the scene Jonathan is not looking at David as a threat. He is looking at David as an answer to his prayer. Jonathan was a man who really loved his people. So when he saw David running towards the giant with nothing in his hand but a sling and a few stones in his hand came back with a tremendous victory carrying the heavy head of this giant and walked back into the camp, Saul went out to meet him. As the King's son Jonathan was standing next to Saul and Jonathan realized and God has answered his prayers.

What is your agenda? Do you want to see deliverance for God's people or are you selfish enough to think only about you? So many times we have our own agendas and the little things that we want to do. So instead of seeing the deliverance of the people, instead of seeing the big picture, if we are only worried about our own agenda . . . God can never use you. God cannot use narrow minded people.

Look at Jonathan's heart. I wish we could raise up a generation like Jonathan's, who could look beyond their selfish interest, look beyond their own agendas and see the big picture and pray earnestly and say, 'Lord do your will in our generation.' Somehow use us but we do not demand anything special from you. We do not care who you use, we do not care how you use us but use us! Because we live in a generation where many Goliaths are rising up. False religions, new age movements—all sorts of Goliaths rising up threaten the people of God. In the midst of all of this, instead of falling on our knees and praying to Lord to use us somewhere, somehow, we are hung up on our own agendas. God looks at us in sadness as he did at King Saul.

So when God raises up somebody and somebody exceeds you—somebody becomes a better preacher than you, somebody becomes a better prayer warrior than you, somebody starts writing and becomes popular, somebody becomes a better signer than you, how do you confront that situation? Are you threatened or do you embrace it, thank God that He is raising up somebody. The Bible says that Jonathan's soul was knit together with David's. Immediately there was a connection and Jonathan realized that this is what he was waiting for. 'All these days, I was all alone. Because I am the King's son I couldn't go against my own father. I am stuck in this system. Not that I don't have a plan in my heart, not that I don't have ideas but I happen to be the King's son so I am stuck in this system. Now together we can do something. We can make sure that God's children can have victory.'

In 1 Samuel 18, verse 4, we read, "and Jonathan took off the robe that was on him." It is not a regular robe. It is a purple robe of a prince, and he is taking it off and handing it over to David. And then he gave David his armor, even to his sword and his bow and his belt. He gave all of his weapons to David in effect saying, "Listen, I see God is going to use you. God has already started using you. I know that God has great plans for you for the future so I am giving you everything I have. Let us work together."

We can see, right there, the heart of Jonathan. But while Jonathan is doing this, in the same chapter we see another character, King Saul, who is threatened by all of this. Let me show you the differences between Saul and Jonathan.

In verses 7 and 8 we see Saul becoming jealous. "So the women sang as they danced and said, 'Saul has slain his thousands and David his ten thousands,' and Saul was very angry. Saying this displeased him. He said, they have ascribed to David ten thousands and to me they have only ascribed only thousands now what more can he have but the kingdom." He becomes jealous right away. For a song! The entire nation was rejoicing. Look at the tragedy, the pathetic situation that King Saul was in. The entire nation was rejoicing except him. He was the King, he should be at the head of that parade rejoicing that God gave them victory. 'God gave us victory let us rejoice, let us rejoice!' Instead of doing that he was threatened by all of this.

That is the problem with inferiority complex. They are threatened by everything. If you are in a situation like that, please note. We are not just repeating a story that is three thousand years old. These are life lessons. If you have that problem of inferiority complex, get over it because your inferiority complex will not change anything. The fact that you complain about everything will change nothing. From morning until night, let us say, you are complaining to your husband or you are complaining to your wife because of the threat you feel in your heart. That changes nothing. The next morning when you wake up you are going to face the same reality all over again. So you better get over it and accept it.

King Saul became very jealous but that was just the beginning. We read in verse 9 that Saul eyed David from that day forward. That means Saul is sending the message, 'I am watching you boy, I know you are able, I know you are capable but I am watching you.' Why all this fuss? Because Saul's desire is that Jonathan should become the next King. But God has already raised up somebody else to be the next King and Jonathan has accepted it.

But Saul cannot accept it. So Saul is suspecting every move of David. It doesn't end there, look at verse 10 it says, And it happened on the next day, that the distressing spirit from God came upon Saul and he prophesied inside the house. So David played music with his hands and at other times there was a spear in Saul's hand and Saul cast the spear and he said, "I will pin David to the wall but David escaped his presence twice." When you get jealous and when you get filled with the inferiority complex, sometimes in the natural we are born that way and we cannot do anything about it. But when you allow the natural conditions to take over you, take hold of you instead of becoming the new creation that Jesus promised, we have missed the point. So many times I have seen this sad story. Even after people have said they gave their heart to Jesus, they refuse to become the new creation that Jesus promised to make them. They still remain the same. It should not be like that!

If we move forward in that new creation process and allow Holy Spirit to transform you, as we read in Romans, chapter 12, verses 1 and 2 by the renewing of our mind, God will take us from where we were at the bottom of the totem pole and bring us up to a level of full stature in Jesus Christ. But instead of allowing the Holy Spirit to do that growth process in us if we get stuck where we were in the natural. Initially Saul thought, 'this is the way I always was. I was always plagued with inferiority complex.' But Saul, you had a change of heart, remember? When Samuel poured out that oil of anointing upon your head, what did the Bible say in the very next verse? He received a new heart! And what happened to that new heart that God gave him? That was supposed to be a new beginning in his life. He was supposed to grow from there. Instead of growing from there he went back to who he was in the natural again and again until he got stuck there. Then he is consumed by fear, he is eyeing people, he is suspicious of everything everyone does, he cannot stand anyone, he cannot rejoice in anyone's victory. You can be inside the church and yet give room for Satan in your life.

The Bible says that the next day a distressing spirit came and started haunting him. All this time he only had to worry about his natural self but now he has to worry about demon possession on top of that! Imagine that! He is already failing in the natural and on top of that a demon enters into his life.

Can Christians be demon possessed? Some people say that once you are a child of God, Satan is afraid of you. It does not matter whatever mess you did after that. No, that's not true! You can become a child of God and later on in your life you can be possessed by demons. But when that happens, God is not sending that demon into your life, you are allowing that demon to enter your life because you refuse to go along with God.

God started something new and beautiful in your life. When you were not worthy of anything, he came and he showed pity on you. He had compassion, he lifted you up from the miry clay of sin, put your feet on the solid rock and said, 'listen child of mine, I have planted you on the rock of ages, now go forward!' Even after God plants you on the rock of ages, and gives you a push in life and says go forward from here you refuse to go with God. You go back to your natural stuff again. And when you say,' but I was always like this,' you negate everything that God did in your life. When you say that you are saying that God did not change me, I did not have a new heart, I did not have a new beginning in my life. Is that true? No, it is not true. It is a lie from the pit of hell and Satan has influenced you enough to believe that lie. Get out of that trap. Do not give room for Satan. Stop swallowing the lies from Satan. Show a little bit of courage to stand on your feet and say, 'No! I may have messed up, I may have failed in my life, I may have failed my Savior but I am a new creation nonetheless. I am a new creation. Jesus started something new in me. When the whole world gave up on me, when the world did not want me, when the world already decreed that I would be a failure, Jesus came and started something new in me. I may not have always gone forward as he expected but nonetheless I am a new creation.' Stop believing the lies of Satan. Otherwise you will end up in Satan's camp. You will have a certificate saying you were baptized on such and such date. You may have a certificate saying you finished Sunday school on such and such date, it does not matter. Satan does not care about that paper. He only cares where your heart is today.

When Saul initially started going away from God he never thought he would be possessed by demons one day. He thought after all I am anointed with the holy oil of God. Anointed by Samuel himself! How can I ever end up as a demon possessed man, it will never happen. But I am dabbling a little bit here and there and I will come back at some point. When you play with God, you are playing with fire. You and I are Christians today only because of the grace of God upon our lives. None of us can stand against Satan in our own strength. He is a roaring lion running around looking for somebody fresh to swallow. Do not put your head in his mouth! Stand up on the word of God, and declare that you are a new creation in Christ.

It did not stop there. Look at verse 12. When Satan enters into you, you know what happens. Jesus said, the thief comes only to kill, rob and destroy. Satan is nobody's friend. As soon as Saul gave room for Satan, he came in. Look at this negative progression in this man's life. He was an anointed man, a King of Israel at one time but look what is happening to him. Initially it was only jealousy and then he became very suspicious, then he could not stand anyone, he could not take part in joy of other people, would not be happy with anyone else. Then slowly, slowly Satan found himself a person whom he could take over in the life of Saul. As soon as Satan took over, we read in verse 12, he became possessed with a spirit or murder. The next thing he did was take the spear and cast it against David and try to pin him against the wall. And that spirit of murder never left King Saul until he killed himself.

For the next few chapters we see him chasing David. Occasionally he will repent. But this evil spirit would come back to him and take over his life and push him to go after David again. And when that demon of murder eventually could not kill David, it induced the mind of Saul to kill himself. Every suicide is not out of depression. Every suicide is not because of financial failure. So many people have gone through financial failures and they have regained more than they lost. People have come back from the pit of depression and today have beautiful lives. Every suicide is not because of a failed love, or a failed marriage or a failed business venture. Sometimes that maybe the case, but I believe many times it happens because there is a spirit that comes over them and induces them to destroy themselves. This demon of murder that came on King Saul pushed him as much as possible to kill David. When they could not do that they turned around and induced the mind of Saul to kill himself, it ended up with murder anyway. When you give room to Satan you better be careful.

Please parents, tell this to your children when they dabble in little things. Maybe it is just the Ouija board or some other video games. You may say how can a game have a demon spirit? The idea came from the sorcerers that is why we say there is evil spirit there. As a result of dabbling in these things, how many children killed their parents or grandparents in recent years? When they are taken to court, they say somebody told us to go and kill grandma. When you start dabbling with evil, when you give room for Satan in your life, watch out! Once he comes in he will not go that easily because he likes to possess things. At one time, he was only second to God in heaven. He lost all of that and he has that sense of loss, and it is bugging him, consuming him. So he always wants to possess something. That is why Satan comes after us. He comes to possess your children, to possess your health, to possess your family, to possess your relationship, to possess your mind. And he will not leave that easily. The best option is never to give room for Satan in your life and your family.

Look at the story in Mark 5. There we see a young man living in a grave yard and morning till night he was taking a stone and cutting himself. When Jesus appeared, in a second he became normal and all that habit disappeared from him. So why was he cutting himself? This is what I think. This was a young man who came from a nice family and he had plenty of material blessings at one time. Initially when he started dabbling with Satan he was pleasing Satan and Satan eventually took over his mind because Satan is possessive and Satan demand worship from the people who become his captive. But now this young man is out of home, out of community running around naked in graveyards and he has nothing to offer. But Satan will not stop just because your pocket is empty. Walk through the streets of Manhattan and meet the homeless people. When you stop to talk to them, you will be surprised that they have college degrees and even master's degrees. So how did they end up like that? In the natural we would look at them and say they have a behavioral problem and all we have to do is take them to a psychologist and they will be fixed. No, no! In that case they would be fixed a long time ago.

You know what happens once you allow Satan to come into your life and your pocket is full of money, Satan will demand that money. Go get more booze, go get more drugs. 'Destroy your mind more and more so that I can take it over completely' and he will continue to lead you into that path until he takes over your mind completely. By that time your pocket is empty. That is when Satan really goes to work he will say, 'Your pocket is empty but you still have to please me. So go rob from your mother, rob from your father, rob from your grandfather. Do not think Satan will stop there either. He may entice you put a brown bag on your head and go to the bank and rob the teller or rob the old woman who is crossing the street. He never stops his demands in your life. And this young man had nothing to give to Satan. Satan was still demanding. The only thing he had left was blood in his veins. He took sharp stones and cut his hand and let the blood flow as an offering to Satan. A few hours later Satan would come oppressing again demanding more and more. He had no peace. He would cut himself again. Do not worry even if you know people who are going through that situation. There is a Jesus who can set them free in a second. If you know somebody that is beyond hope, beyond professional help, bring them to Jesus. Jesus can set their life back to order.

Saul became possessed by a murderous spirit. And the same in verse 12, the last sentence says that he became afraid of David. In verse 25, we can see that he started manipulating to kill David but it did not end there. Listen, if you are a David you do not have to worry. This entire kingdom is trying to finish off this young man but they cannot touch him. If God is raising you up nobody can touch you! That is why later David wrote this beautiful Psalm where he said, 'A thousand may fall at your side, And ten thousand at your right hand; But it shall not come near you.' (Psalms 91:7). If God is for you who can be against you? If God is on your side, who can hunt you down? No one! No weapon that is fashioned against you shall prosper.

CHAPTER V

Power of a Covenant

In the previous chapter, we were looking at the unique relationship that David and Jonathan had. We saw that Jonathan was a very unusual person because he was supposed to be the heir apparent; he was supposed to be the next King. Here was God raising somebody up to take the throne away from him but nonetheless he never complained. Instead he looked at David as an answer to his own prayers because he wanted deliverance for his people. Now we compared that with the attitude of his father. We saw that his father on the other hand became very jealous. He knew that if David comes up his son will not become King and he started suspecting every move of David and eventually allowed room for Satan in that process to enter into his life and became possessed with a murderous spirit. And in the end he ended up killing himself.

When you give room for Satan in your life, it is an extremely dangerous. Many times young people without understanding the gravity of it start dabbling in things. How many young lives have been destroyed because they gave room for Satan in their life! And that is where we ended the chapter. I want to come back to Jonathan and David again since there is a lot more to be learned from this unique friendship.

Here we will be focusing on the power of a covenant. We know that their relationship was cemented in 1Samuel, chapter18, after the victory David had over Goliath, when he came back victorious. They made a covenant between themselves and said we will never fight among ourselves. Jonathan came forward and said, "I can see that God is raising you up. I know it is at my expense but nonetheless you are the one whom God is raising up." That is a question that we all have to answer at some point in our life. So Jonathan, being a godly man, realizes that God is raising David and he was okay with that because more than his selfish interest, he was interested in the deliverance of God's people and the nation of Israel. So he said, 'I will enter into a covenant with you and I will always take the second place. You can go forward even though I am supposed to be the next King. God's hand is upon you and I know that God has already manifested his anointing upon your life. So I'm not going to compete with that. I will take the second place and let you go forward.' And they entered into a covenant.

In the Old Testament, when the word covenant was introduced to us, the Hebrew word and the Aramaic word means where the blood flows. The way they entered into a covenant was by cutting an animal and walking between the split animals. In Genesis 15, you can see a picture of that. So blood was always present when they made a covenant. So when David and Jonathan entered into a covenant it means that they became blood brothers.

Do I have to explain? As soon as I say blood brothers, you understand what that means. It means each of them is committed to protect the other one. We can see that process taking place in 1 Samuel 19. In that chapter, immediately Jonathan started protecting David. He knew his father was jealous of David and he knew his father wanted to kill David. So we see in chapter19, Jonathan speaking good things about David. But his father did not want to see David. Jonathan was trying to gain access for David into King Saul's palace again.

Then we see in 1 Samuel 20 that Jonathan became very upset with the way his father treated David. Jonathan says, "My father has treated you shamefully." The father is trying to protect Jonathan in his own mind. But Jonathan thinks he is standing against God and against the move of God and he has treated David shamefully and therefore he was grieving. We see that his father asked him to be selfish in I Samuel 20:30. Saul's anger was aroused against Jonathan. Why? Because Jonathan is supporting David. And this is what his father told him, "you son of a perverse, rebellious woman, do I not know that you have chosen the son of Jesse to your own shame, and to the shame of your mother; for as long as the son of Jesse lives on the earth, you shall not be established nor your kingdom. Now repent and bring him to me for he shall surely die."

The father is asking Jonathan, 'how dumb are you? Don't you know if David is around you will never become King? Don't you know that he is going to come and take the throne away from you? You are dumb enough to support him? So wake up, because he is coming up and going to take your throne and you're going to be out. So wake up and be a little more selfish.' But Jonathan never bought that message because he never saw David as a threat. He saw David as an answer to his prayer. Therefore, this is what we read in verses 41-42, "as soon as the lad had gone, David arose from the place toward the south, fell on his face to the ground and bowed down three times until they kissed one another and wept together." That is covenant brothers!

Then Jonathan said to David, 'Go in peace since we have both sworn in the name of the Lord.' That means, "We have made a covenant. May the Lord be between you and me, between your descendants and my descendants forever." So he arose and departed and Jonathan went into the city. All Jonathan did was renewing the covenant.

Every time they met together they renewed the covenant. In 1 Samuel 23:16-18, which is the last time they saw each other alive and this is what happened: "Then Jonathan, Saul's son, rose and went to David in the woods and strengthened his hand in God." You know when this is happening? His father is chasing David to kill him. Jonathan is in the army, the father and the entire army is looking for David to kill him and Jonathan took a side step and went into the woods where David was hiding and strengthened his hand. That is the power of a covenant!

And he said to him, "Do not fear for the hand of Saul my father shall not find you. You shall be King over Israel and I shall be next to you. Even my father knows that." So the two of them made a covenant before the Lord again and David stayed in the woods and Jonathan went to his own house.

David started running here and there to escape from the hand of King Saul. And eventually Saul and Jonathan ended up in the mountains of Gilboa, where they were in another battle and in that battle both of them were killed. So David never saw Jonathan after the incident in 1 Samuel 23. So in the last three references that we have about their meeting, they did only one thing—they renewed the covenant.

When we come into the presence of God, when we come to worship God do you know what you are doing? You are renewing the covenant in your life. So many times people say, 'what is the big deal about going to a church, why can't I just stay home and watch a message on the TV? Why can't I stay home and open my Bible and read it? I do not need to go to a church. I do not need to attend a service.' Let me tell you something, every time you come into the presence of God, you are renewing the covenant between you and God. When you are in church, you are in the midst of a covenant community.

Do you believe there is a covenant between you and God? Yes, there is a covenant between you and God. When you became a child of God, He entered into a covenant with you. The covenant was established 2,000 years ago when He died on the cross for the sake of the entire mankind. When he shed his precious blood for the sins of mankind, the covenant was established. Today what He does is he grafts you into that established covenant. So you have a portion in that same covenant! All of us are part of that same covenant. What is that covenant? The covenant of the cross! The day you became a child of God you became a part of that covenant but you have to renew that covenant in your life.

Look at Jonathan; he knew the value of the covenant. At one point he expected that would be a lifelong friendship. 'Eventually my father will cool down and my father will die and I will step aside and let David be King and I will just be his prime minister.' But that's not the way things played out.

A few chapters later Jonathan is dead in that battle. But before he died, as long as he was alive, every opportunity he got, he renewed the covenant. When you get up early in the morning, when you find a little time to pray to God in the midst of a busy schedule, when you know you are a little late and you may miss that train or you may catch the traffic on the Long Island Expressway or Southern State Parkway whichever highway you use, you can still you say, 'Lord I want to put you first in my life. I'm going to take a couple of minutes, and pray before I step out of my house.' When you do that, for that day a covenant is renewed in your life and you will have God's protection upon your life. You will have God's covering upon your life so nothing will touch you during that day. A covenant is a very powerful thing.

What about the covenant after Jonathan is dead? A covenant is never forgotten. Look at these things that will touch your heart. Look at 2Samuel 1:17, 18. David knew that he had made a covenant, and that covenant was supposed to last not only between him and Jonathan but also between their descendants. So even though Jonathan is gone, David did not want to forget Jonathan. "Then David lamented with the lamentation of Saul and over Jonathan his son and he told them to teach the children of Judah the song of the Bow; indeed it was written in the book of Jasher who was a musician in that generation."

David is desperately trying to keep the memory of Jonathan alive. Let me show you the fruits of that covenant relationship. The first thing was this: Even though Jonathan was dead, David did not say he is dead I am King now so I do not have to worry about anything. That was then and this is now. No! That is a utilitarian mindset and we know that we live in a world with a utilitarian mindset.

How easily people forget others, people who prayed for them, people who stood with them, people who supported them, people who lent them a hand. As soon as we hit the good times we always forget them. We do not want to waste our time thinking about them. We live in a small world.

But in a midst of a world like that David sets a different example. He says, 'Jonathan, you were cut off in the middle of your life, but I will do my best to make sure your memory stays alive.' David being a musician (and music has more power, because people can remember those lines) he wrote a special song, the song is given to us as a Psalm. He wrote a Psalm just for Jonathan and he told all of Israel to learn that song and sing that song. He appointed a musician to make sure that people were taught the song again and again so that Jonathan's memory will remain fresh. Covenant is powerful!

It doesn't end there. Turn to 2Samuel 9:1. *Now David said, "Is there still anyone who is left of the house of Saul that I may show him kindness for Jonathan's sake?"* He sent out his servants to find out if there was anyone at all alive so that he may show mercy for Jonathan's sake.

There was a servant of the house of Saul whose name was Ziba. When they had called him to David the King said to him, 'Are you Ziba?' and he said, 'At your service!' Then the king said "Is there not still someone of the house of Saul to whom I may show the kindness of God?" And Ziba said to the king "There is still a son of Jonathan who is lame in his feet." So the king said to him "Where is he?" And Ziba said to the king "Indeed he is in the house of Machir the son of Ammiel in Lo Debar." Then King David sent and brought him out of the house of Machir the son of Ammiel from Lo Debar. Now when Mephibosheth the son of Jonathan the son of Saul had come to David he fell on his face and prostrated himself. Then David said "Mephibosheth?" And he answered "Here is your servant!" So David said to him "Do not fear for I will surely show you kindness for Jonathan your father's sake and will restore to you all the land of Saul your grandfather; and you shall eat bread at my table continually." Then he bowed himself and said "What is your servant that you should look upon such a dead dog as I?" (2 Sam. 9:2-8)

Do you know what is happening there? In the old days the incoming King never showed mercy to the children of the previous King. Because if any descendants of the previous King was alive, they could be a threat for their kingdom or their throne. So as soon as someone new comes on the throne they will wipe out the generations of the previous King. So naturally when people told Mephibosheth that David is looking for him, he was scared so he ran away to a place called Lo Debar. A place of nothing, where nothing grows—that is what it literally means. Living dried up, just a mere existence, somehow trying to stay away from the eyes of David.

When he was brought into the presence of David that is why he prostrated himself, that is why he was actually asking for mercy. Because the King could kill him. He did not know what the intentions of the King were. But the King said, 'You were not brought into my presence to be killed. You were brought into the presence so that you can receive the blessings of the covenant that I made with your father Jonathan.'

The Bible tells us that none of us were worthy to worship God. We were far away from the commonwealth of Israel. Far away from the blessings of God, there was nothing good in us. The Bible declares no one is righteous and that we were all unrighteous, we were all fit to be judged and to go straight to hell. So when God comes seeking for us we get scared like Mephibosheth because we are always worried about the judgment that should naturally fall upon us. But now when God calls upon you, He has a separate message for you. He says, 'I am not looking for you to judge you or to kill you or finish you off, but to make sure that you get your inheritance in the covenant that I made on behalf of you with my son Jesus Christ!'

Mephibosheth said, 'I'm nothing but a dead dog.' That's the right attitude when we come into the presence of God. We are not worthy of walking into the presence of King of Kings, Lord of Lords. But nonetheless he invites us into his presence. That is why the Psalm says, 'Blessed is the man whom God has chosen to dwell in his presence.' We cannot go into his presence unless He invites us. He has invited us! So he showed mercy to Mephibosheth, who was a lame boy. All of his life he lived with nothing. Even though he was a prince, he was living as a destitute in a far away land. Look at his privileges now!

Look at the spiritual connotations of this story. The prince is living as a destitute in a far away land where nothing grows . . . the King is sending people to find him there and bring him into the royal palace and gave him a permanent seat on the Kings table. Isn't that what God has done for us? God created us to rule the earth. God created us to live like princes. God created us to live in the bounty of his blessings but because of the presence of sin in our life we walked away from that, we were in a far away land. We were living like destitute having nothing, no presence of God, nothing good in us. When we thought He would just push our days like that until death comes calling one day, He sent someone to fetch us out from there. Not only that he fetched us out, he brought us into the palace and has given you a permanent seat (not a temporary, but a permanent seat) on the Kings table!

Let me show you one more thing about covenant. In 2 Samuel 21, you can see David sparing the life of Mephibosheth. A lot of things happened in between which we will cover later. Mephibosheth was a person like us. How many times after getting the privilege of having our sins washed away, getting access into the presence of God, seeing so many of our prayers answered, have we backslided and gone away from God? Can you believe that Mephibosheth turned against David one day? That is the total depravity of human nature.

When Absalom, one of David's sons, got up in a revolt against his own father, David had to run away from the palace. A lot of people followed David. You can see very old people following David. Strangers were following David out of sympathy towards him. But this young man who was in the pit of depression, in the pit of nothing, from where David went and fetched him out and brought him to the table and gave him a permanent seat on the table, did not go with him. When David fell on hard times, he changed the tone and said, 'Now the kingdom will come back to me because one day it was supposed to come to me as Jonathan's son.' A picture of total depravity of human nature!

When David was coming back in chapter 21, at the end of that saga, David showed mercy to Mephibosheth again. There's a statement that David told Mephibosheth. 'You should have been dead today but because of the covenant I made with Jonathan, I am sparing your life.'

How many times have we walked away from God after knowing God? Forget about the times we did not know God. Even after knowing God, even after tasting and seeing He is good, how many of us have we walked away from him? We did not deserve a second chance. How many times did God give you a second chance, a third chance, a fourth chance, a fifth chance, and a sixth chance? Do you know why? Have you ever wondered why? Why does God still love you? Why God has not consumed you? He could have sent one lightening and finished us off but why didn't He? If you ask God that question, there is only one answer. He will say, 'Because I made a covenant on your behalf. You are part of a covenant. I cannot forget you.'

Let us look at a verse in the New Testament. "Now may the God of peace who brought up our Lord Jesus from the dead the great shepherd of the sheep through the blood of the everlasting covenant make you complete in every good work to do His will." (Hebrews 13:20). Do you know why you get mercy again and again? Because you are part of an everlasting covenant! God doesn't change his covenant every time we do something wrong. Please do not use it as a license to do wrong again and again in your life. But the Bible says, 'if you sin He is faithful and just to forgive us.'

Do you know why He forgives again? Because of the everlasting covenant His Son made on our behalf. If it was a temporary covenant, we would have all been destroyed a long time ago including me. I am not writing this with an attitude that I am better than you. I'm not. All of us would have been finished off a long time ago. But God loved us with an everlasting covenant and because of this He forgives us again and again.

Do you have that confidence in your life that God has made you a part of that everlasting covenant? If you do not, you can never enter into His blessings and forgiveness. I want you to use this occasion to enter into that covenant. If you are part of that covenant and have been walking away from it in the past or in recent times, I want you to come back into your place in that covenant because that covenant He made with you is everlasting. You may have forgotten all about it, but God takes it seriously. The covenant that He made with you is an everlasting covenant. You are part of that everlasting covenant today and He is waiting for you to come back to Him.

So this was more than a friendship, it was a covenant relationship. That is where we can identify with David and Jonathan. We saw the power of the covenant in the way David was dealing with Jonathan's generation. We saw how Mephibosheth became a privileged person only because of the covenant that David made with his father in which Mephibosheth had nothing to do. So all the blessings that we have today, all the blessings in the heavenly places that are ours today have nothing to do with us. It is not our good works, it is not our efforts, it is not what we do but it is because of the covenant that was made on the cross two thousand years ago.

When Mephibosheth came back after going away from the covenant in the sense that he stayed away from David for a while, he was put in the same seat again. Even though he did that wicked thing in his life, even though he did that crazy stuff he was put back in that same seat all over again. That is what God wants to do with your life. God wants to restore you. He wants to put you back into that covenant, the place that you enjoyed one time in your life, when you used to walk close with God.

Remember the days when you used to walk close with God? Remember the days when you knew that you were grafted into this covenant? Remember the time when you had that confidence every time you prayed, every time you opened the Bible? Every time you walked into a service you walked in with confidence that I am a child of God, I am part of this covenant and I belong here. If that is lost in your life I want you take this opportunity to renew that covenant once again. He is a gracious God. Just as David put Mephibosheth back into his permanent seat, God wants to bring you back into the place where you belong. He wants to bring you back into the destiny that He originally designed for you.

CHAPTER VI

What if God Asks You To Wait?

What we are learning through these studies is that you do not wake up one fine morning and become a man or a woman after God's own heart. It is actually a process and it takes time to get to that level. In this chapter, we will focus on chapter 20 and 21 of 1Samuel 20 and 21 and learn lessons from a tough period in David's life.

We have meditated on the covenant relationship that David and Jonathan established and saw that Saul was bent on destroying David because Saul can see that God is raising up David, and just like any other father, he wanted to take care of his son. So he knew if David is coming up like this I am going to have a problem later. My son Jonathan cannot become the King in the land. So the father decided to kill David before he gets the throne. But on the other hand, Jonathan had no problem with what God was doing. Jonathan had the mindset of a true child of God. But the father couldn't accept that. The father wanted the throne to remain in the family so even though David was his own son-in-law that is not the way he was looking at David. And therefore he was bent on destroying David. He already made many attempts but we see that the attempts failed. Then David had to run out because every time this man sees David he gets enraged. Now Saul is filled with a demonic presence in his life and every time he sees David who is filled with the Holy Spirit something begins to boil in the life of King Saul (who lost the presence of Holy Spirit) and he will take a spear and try to kill him. Every time he sees David, every time he thinks about David he becomes enraged and that murderous spirit will come and take over Saul's life. So we know that David had to get out of there because David was no longer feeling comfortable staying in that palace even though he's the son-in-law of the King. So he is running here and there trying to minimize his exposure to this King who is demon possessed now.

At the same time, David got used to the luxuries of living in a palace. Remember a while ago, David was living in the wilderness, even his own parents did not care about him but it did not bother him. He got so used to that lifestyle in the wilderness, he was a happy go lucky guy, he would grab some honey or just grab an animal and kill it and eat it and he would sleep under a tree, it was no problem. He would still write songs and take his harp and worship God. He was comfortable with that lifestyle. But once he became a King's son-in-law, and started living in the palace, it became very hard to give up that lifestyle. Let me remind you once again, we are not just reiterating a story that is three thousand years old, we are actually talking about practical things we can relate to.

Why do we end up in a lot of credit card debt, especially during an economic downturn like this? You hear stories after stories of people who are $30,000, $40,000, $50,000 in credit card debt. Do you think anyone enjoys being in debt? No one enjoys being in debt. Do you think these people do not know what they are doing? Yes they know. But sometimes they get caught up in this syndrome. Ten years ago when I was driving a fifteen year old Chevy, it was ok. If I only had $5 in my pocket it was fine because I knew how to manage my life with $5. But then I got a nice job paying me $80,000 a year and I went out and bought a Lexus and I decided to buy a home for myself and I got all these things laid out there and I have to have 'x' amount of dollars coming in each month to maintain my lifestyle which I was comfortable with. Especially some young couples these days make a lot of money and that comfortable lifestyle in the suburb with a nice couple of cars looks good. Despite monthly payments and big utility bills, I mean you get used to all the luxuries of life. One day when the luxury is taken away from you in the form of one of you getting laid off, very few people will say, 'let's sell this house and move back to an apartment. And when God brings this provision back into our life we will buy another house.' I know wise people who do that but most people are not that wise. So what do we do? First of all, we don't want anyone to know that we are struggling. Secondly, you have an image to maintain, remember we talked about that. And when your emphasis becomes maintaining your image, you are in trouble. So in order to maintain the image, what do you do? You pull out one plastic card after another. As soon as they see you are using one plastic card after another they will send you ten more. And you say, 'thank you Lord! I got ten more credit cards now.' Before you know you have $50,000 in credit balance. What are you going to do with $50,000 credit balance? You can never run this out, you think. It will last forever. And you keep pulling that card out and in no time you will certainly end up in $50,000 credit card debt. Why, because you want to maintain your image? You want to maintain that lifestyle. Not because we enjoy credit card debt but we don't want to give up that standard of living.

Then one fine morning, you realize that you cannot even make the minimum payment on all of this. And the calls start coming in. People start harassing you and they take off your cell phone. You are out there chilling out with your friends and the collection agency calls. Then it becomes public that you are struggling. None of us want to go through that. This is a sad truth. So many millions of people are going through this country because we get used to certain standard of living. And that is exactly where David was.

David was sleeping under a tree one time and it did not matter. When he wrote in Psalm 23, 'he lay me down on green pastures,' that was not a figure of speech. That is where he used to sleep. It did not matter to him. He said, 'the Lord is my shepherd, I shall not want.' That means I don't need anything more than this. I am happy with what he has given to me in my life. But then David became the King's son-in-law. Choice meals three times a day, a luxury bed to sleep on and all the other amenities that comes with that lifestyle. Then one day all of a sudden, it started disappearing.

What do you do when things don't go the way you expect them to go? How do you handle your life? How do you handle that challenge? David had tremendous approval from the public. If you look at 1 Samuel, chapter 19, you see that people loved him. He already has become a captain of 1,000 soldiers, he's the King's son-in-law, and there are multiple privileges that come with that. He was already being recognized as the sweet singer of Israel, and all the public accolades that comes with that. And then he was made the captain of 1,000 soldiers and he was getting respect from the military. All these things add up. So we can see that David is slowly settling down in his life and beginning to enjoy the good life. Then all of a sudden, God started taking that out.

At the beginning of chapter 20 we can see fear entering into the life of this man of God. He comes to Jonathan and says, 'What did I do wrong? What did I do against your father? I am his son-in-law, why is he treating me like this?' In effect, he was actually requesting Jonathan to find a way for him to go back to the palace. He is sending a message that 'I don't like running around anymore. It was okay at one time in my life, I don't want to live a hard life anymore. I am supposed to be in the palace, I know there is a bed for me in the palace. I want to go back there. Can you help me to find a way to get back there?'

Fear and faith do not go along. Fear is the killer of faith. If you allow fear to enter into your life, I don't care how anointed you are, how long you have been a Christian, how wonderful you are being used by God, if you allow fear to enter into your life your life will go down. It will kill the faith in your life and your outlook will change. Your assessment about your life will change. Look at chapter 20 and verse 3. This is David's assessment about his own situation: "there is but one step between me and death." What a dire assessment about his life! He does not believe that what is happening in his life at that particular juncture is with the knowledge of God. He does not believe any longer that God is in control of his life. He no longer believes that God is directing him in a certain way. He thinks something has happened to his relationship with God. Somehow God has forgotten about him. 'I know all this time God was interested in me. I didn't want to become a King! God is the one who found me and anointed me. I did not go after the anointing; he found me and anointed me. I did not look for Goliath; God is the one who presented Goliath over there so people can see that there is an anointing upon me. God is the one who gave me that victory. After sending me up this ladder for some reason he is pulling the ladder from under my feet. That's the way David is looking at his life now.

In 1 Samuel 22:3, you can see another dire assessment of David of his own life. This is what he told a gentile King. This is a man of God going to a gentile King with his parents and leaving his parents with the gentile King because he is afraid that Saul will kill them also. And when he left his parents with this gentile King this is what we read, "And David went from there to Mespah of Moab, and he said to the King of Moab, and please let my father and mother come here with you *till I know what God will do for me*". Every time I read that statement, I can completely identify with David. David is saying, 'I have no clue what God is doing with my life.' If you are truthful, how many times we have been there? How many times we have looked at our life and said, 'I don't know what's going on in my life? Please don't ask me for an explanation, I have no explanation for you.'

And David is going to the King of Moab, a gentile King and saying I don't know what God is doing with me. The King is probably asking, 'Why are you bringing your parents here? Aren't you a Jew? Why did you come to a gentile King for the protection of your parents?' And David had no explanation. David probably said, 'if I knew I would tell you. Please let them stay here until I can come back with an explanation. Right now I have no clue what God is doing in my life. How many of you are in that juncture in your life?

Be truthful to yourself. We don't need to pretend anything before God. He sees us as we are. He knows our thoughts; he knows our sitting down and rising up. There is absolutely nothing that is hidden from his eyes. Haven't we all said from time to time, "Lord, what are you doing with me, what are you doing in my life? I have no idea Lord. You are supposed to be my heavenly father. You are supposed to be in charge of my welfare but things are not going the way I expected. All I see is struggles after struggles. I cannot come up with an explanation for where I am today, for what I am going through in my life today.' If that is where you are, I want you to be truthful before God today.

These are times that test us. To talk about a faithful God all the time and then one fine morning all of a sudden wake up in the midst of a whole set of problems realizing that God has not come through for me. I don't know if you have been there, I have been there. If you ask my wife, she will tell you how many days I was waking up 2 o'clock, 3 o'clock in the morning and walking around in the house praying silently because I could not go to sleep. She was forced to get up and she would ask 'what's wrong, what's wrong?' And I couldn't tell her what's wrong. I would say, 'nothing, you go back to sleep.' And you are pacing the house asking, 'Lord why is this thing happening in my life? Why I find myself in this condition? How come you don't speak to me? I can suffer the problems; I can handle the problems if you talk to me. At least talk to me and tell me, come put your hands on my shoulder and give me a little bit of assurance and say son you're going to go through this for six months then you will be out. And that will be fine with me; I will suffer for six months.' Sometimes he does not do that. It feels like you are left in the dark alone and you feel like I have wasted my time talking about the faithfulness of God all of these years. Preaching from so many stages about the faithfulness of God and then to find myself . . . There will be seasons like that in your life. Every day of your life will not be rosy.

Martin Luther, the father of reformation, went through a season like that in his life. He could not sleep at night. Every night he would be pacing back and forth and his wife put up with that for a while. And then one night he was pacing in his living room and his wife came to him and said, 'Martin I have news for you.' He said what? 'Your God is dead.' Martin said, 'No way! My God is an eternal God! He cannot die.' So finally this wise woman said,' but you are not acting like that. You are acting like your God is dead.' That changed his life. When you go through tough times in your life, when you do not see the rainbow showing up in the midst of the clouds in your life, the signs of the covenant do not manifest in your life, remember, He is still on the throne.

As you continue in that chapter, David went to Jonathan and said, find a way for me to come back to the palace because I don't want to live the hard life again. Now Jonathan, because he was a covenant brother said, Give me three days and I will go back to the palace and I will watch my father to see how he is acting. The next day was a thanksgiving day and they were supposed to have a big dinner and David's chair was empty. The first day Saul was quiet, he didn't make a big scene about it. The second day he said, 'Where is the son of Jesse, how come I don't see him here?' And Jonathan said, 'There is a celebration going on in his own house so he asked me permission to go there.' And by the third day, this man got so enraged and the evil presence in him began to manifest. So Jonathan said, 'Why do you get so upset about David, what did he do wrong? He is a wonderful guy, he's your son-in-law.' But he got so angry that he tried to kill his own son. Then Jonathan knew that this man will stop at nothing until he killed David.

Jonathan had told David to hang out just three days in the wilderness and on the third day I want you to come to a particular stone (the stone of Essel) that simply means "the stone." But I want to call it the stone of destiny because David was waiting there by that stone for three days. What do you think David was doing for those three days? David would be doing exactly any of us who are children of God would be doing. And this was the thing that they agreed upon. Jonathan said, 'After three days I will come. You wait here by the stone and I will come with a servant of mine as if I am doing target practice. I will shoot some arrows, watch where the arrows are going to land.' Let's

What do you think David was doing there for three days? He was on his knees praying and fasting. What is the topic of the prayer? 'Lord, you are my God I have been serving you faithfully so I know at the end of three days Jonathan is coming back with the servant and he's going to shoot that arrow and he told me if the arrow falls in front of the stone that means everything is okay and I can go back to the palace. But if the arrows go beyond the stone and falls on the other side it means that things are not going good you better get out of here. My father is going to kill you. Lord, let the arrow fall in front of the stone. You are an almighty God; you can make all things possible. Let the arrow fall in front of the stone, Lord.' Fasting and praying for three days and he probably told everyone who came by, 'I know I have been praying. I have prayed so many times before in the past and every time I prayed good things happened. God will hear my prayer. I am pretty sure the arrow is going to fall in the front of this stone.'

Then the designated time came and he heard the voice of Jonathan who was purposely shouting so David can hear. Jonathan called the servant and said, 'Here, I am going to shoot the arrow, pick up the arrow and come back.' And David is anxiously waiting by the stone praying probably afraid to open his eyes and look. And praying, 'Lord you are my God, I am your servant. I'm pretty sure you will cause the arrow to fall in front of the stone so I can go back to the palace.' And while David was praying, he heard the sound of the arrow swishing above his head and falling way beyond where he was waiting. What do you do when God does that to you?

Here you are praying, praying, praying expectantly praying believing and probably proclaiming every faith statement in the Bible, quoting all the scriptures that you know, but the arrow went above your head and fell far beyond where you expected it to fall. What do you do? What was the message? 'God is sending you away so go in peace.'

Basically Jonathan was telling David, this is an unexpected season in your life, things are not going the way you expected but don't give up on God. Even though you are in the midst of this season, trust in God because you are the one who told me trust in God. Remember you are the one who taught me the songs that talked about the faithfulness of God. So don't give up on God, go in peace. Go with the peace of God because this season won't last forever in your life.

And they renewed the covenant and Jonathan went to the palace and David had to leave. Some of you are seated by that stone today, waiting expectantly for an answer. Many of us are praying about different things and looking at God for an answer.

What do you do when the answer doesn't come as you expect, how will you handle it? Will you have the peace of God in your life or will you let fear take over your life?

Do you know what the most tragic chapter in David's life is? It is 1Samuel 21. That chapter tells us explicitly what will happen to each one of us if we are unwilling to accept God's plan for our life. When we make plans for ourselves and when we seek the acknowledgement of God, the approval of heaven for our plans, God changes that plan because He is a sovereign God and he takes authority over your life and my life and will say, 'I know these are the plans you made for your life but I am changing it. Because I am the sovereign God, I am your Lord so I can take that authority.' Without asking permission from us, sometimes He comes and just established His sovereignty over our lives and sends us in a different direction than we expect. That is the toughest time in the life of a child of God. And that is when your faith will really show its depth. When things are going good, it is easy to write songs, it is easy to sing songs, it is easy to lead worship, it is easy to get up on a stage and preach. It is easy to go out and tell people about the faithfulness of God. But when things are going wrong in your life, which is when the true depth of your faith will manifest.

David was a man of God; there is no doubt about that. Nonetheless, when God sent him away, when Jonathan told him about entering into a different season in his life, David could not accept it. When Jonathan said, 'Don't question God, just stay with God. Go with the peace of God, maintain the peace of God in your life,' David could not.

We say 1 Samuel 21 is a dark chapter in the life of David because we see him running. He has no idea what to do next. This was the same man who said, 'that though thousands camp by my side, and ten thousands camp by my right side, I shall not be afraid.' The same man who said, "I will fear no evil, thy rod is with me, thy rod will comfort me.' There are faith statements in every song he wrote up to that point. But now he is running. Because he has this feeling that God has given up on him.

He thought he needed to care of himself. He started running to the tribe of Benjamin, to a city called Noab. That is where the tabernacle was at that time and he ran into it probably seeking shelter and refuge because he feels that somebody is following him and he was hungry for many days. He went into that tabernacle and there were priests and their family members, altogether 86 people. The first thing he asked is, is there something to eat, I'm so hungry. The Levites ate whatever people gave them so when this man ran into that tabernacle that day and met the priests there, they had nothing to offer him. The priest said, 'there is nothing here to eat except the shew bread.' That is the bread they put in the arc every Sabbath day. The next Sabbath day they will put new bread in there. And they had just changed the bread so the priest said this is the only thing we have here. There is nothing else to eat for 86 people.

But David now feels that I must take care of myself because God is no longer taking care of me so he went and said, 'can I have that?' And they said, 'only priests are allowed to eat this bread you must be holy, otherwise you cannot eat this. God will reject you.' And David started lying.

Look at what happens to a child of God who doesn't accept God's dealing with his or her life. This man of God started lying. The first question they asked was 'how come you are alone?' You are the captain of 1,000 troops, when you come you are not supposed to come alone, somebody should be there with you. And he said, 'they are just there waiting outside.' He started lying to the priests in the very presence of God! Right inside the tabernacle he started lying! And secondly the priests said, 'You cannot eat this bread unless you are pure or sanctified.' He said, 'We are sanctified, even though women are with us, we have not slept with our women for the past three days so we are sanctified.' (Remember. David was running away alone and there were no women with him at that point). So he took the bread from them.

He also asked them if they had any weapons. Where is he looking for weapons? Inside the tabernacle! Inside the place of worship, he is looking for weapons. And they said, 'you know we are priests, we don't carry weapons! This is a place of worship.' But David again asked them, "Are you sure there is no weapons here?' They said, 'Well there is one weapon here. The sword that belonged to Goliath at one time. Remember you had that tremendous victory over Goliath? You came to the temple and consecrated that sword as an offering to God to commemorate your victory. Because it's an offering to God we keep it inside.' And David said, 'give it back to me I need it because God is no longer protecting me. I need to protect myself.' Can you imagine a man of God taking back the offering that he gave to God? This is what happens when you cannot trust God anymore. When you think you are in charge of you and you need to take care of yourself. And he took that offering back and he grabbed the bread and started running before they asked any more questions.

He ended up in a city called Gath. Gath was the birthplace of Goliath. David is thinking that was many years ago, I was nothing but a little lad when I had that victory so the people will not recognize me, since now I am an adult. In I Samuel 17, when he killed Goliath, he was a ruddy boy, which means he did not have a beard. Now he is a mature man and he has a beard (Jewish men always had a beard), so David thinks nobody will recognize him. But when he got to Gath, everyone recognized him.

He went straight to the King. It's strange to see that the King accepted him. Because probably, if Goliath was alive, this King would have never become the King. Probably the King was grateful to David for killing Goliath. So he was ready to accept David and let him stay for a while but the people said no. All the people recognized David and said, 'this is the man that killed our hero and you are entertaining him in your palace? Get him out of here, we are going to kill him.' And the people started rising up. I am pretty sure all the mothers in that city were talking about David for a long time. This little Jewish boy was able to kill that great big giant among us because his God is a true living God. All these young people grew up wondering, who is David? What does he look like? We want to see him one day. What made him overcome our giant? And they are waiting for David to meet him. They probably thought they would meet him in a battlefield one day again.

But David showed up among them. And initially they were looking at him as the big hero but then David realized that he is in trouble. People were rising up against him and they were going to kill him. So David started acting like a lunatic. The Bible says, 'he started spitting and the spit started running down his beard and he started babbling with the spit running down.' People would ask, 'are you David?' and he would start babbling. They would ask, 'Are you the one who killed Goliath?' and he would babble again with the spit running down his beard. The King looked at him and said, 'this is the guy who killed the giant? He is a mental patient. Maybe there was no surprise he was able to kill Goliath, probably it was at the climax of one of these episodes that he ran like a madman to our giant and somehow luckily the stone hit him in the forehead and he was able to kill him.' (Paraphrased)

What happened? David lost his testimony in front of the people that feared him all these years for what he did. God lost the glory of that tremendous victory over Goliath because of the same man who was used by God to bring that victory now acted like a lunatic. He is completely taken over by fear. When you allow fear to take over your life, not only that it destroys you, it destroys God's kingdom. It does affect your testimony. It reduces the glory of God because people no longer see a confident man or woman of God who is proclaiming the name of God. And people say, 'this is the guy who was being used by God?' We bring shame to God when we refuse to trust in Him. So finally, the King said, 'Get out before the people come and kill you, get out! The King got so angry and said, 'Don't I have enough mental patients in this country! When did we start importing mental patients from Judah to my country? Get him out of here.'

David got out and he ran to the mountain ranges of Judah. And he started hiding in caves of that area called Adulaam. When you go to Israel you can still see those mountain ranges and caves where people can hide. *That was the hiding place that God had designated for David during that season in his life.* Even when things do not go the way you expect it to go, if you ever enter into a tough season in your life, remember that God has a hiding place for you. That is what Jonathan was telling David. 'David, this is a different season in your life. I do not have any explanation; you do not have any explanation, but don't give up on God. Your God knows how to take care of you even in the midst of this tough season. God has provisions for you. Just go with God, stay with God and enjoy the peace of God and God will hide you in his pavilion.' The place that God had prepared for David for this season of his life was the caves of Adulaam.

When David was not ready to go with God and went to Noab, eventually Saul found that out. And Saul got very angry. Saul went with his soldiers over to the city of Noab to find out where David went from there. And in his rage he killed 85 out of 86 people with his sword. All the priests and their family members including children were killed because of fear in the heart of one man of God who could not believe God. He couldn't accept the provisions that God had for him. Eighty five innocent people died and only one escaped.

Finally when he got to Adullam, he realized that God had a plan for him all the while. The good thing about a child of God is this, eventually you will understand your mistakes. And despite your mistakes God keeps you alive. Despite all the things that David did, God kept him alive and brought him to the hiding place that he had for him. Then he started writing songs again. There are two Psalms in the Bible that David wrote during this time period. The first one is Psalm 56. Look at what he says in verse 3, "Whenever I'm afraid, I will trust in you". He acknowledges that I was taken over by fear, Lord I am ashamed of the things I did. Ashamed of the steps I took, I'm ashamed of the detours I made in my life instead of fully trusting in you. I should have trusted in you. Finally when he came back to his sense, he said, "Whenever I am afraid I will trust in you." In verse four, he says, "I will not fear, what flesh can do to me." And in verse 12, he talks about the vows he made. The vows that I made to you are binding. That means, while he was acting like a madman to fool the people in Gath, in his heart he was praying and making vows to God. And he says, 'Lord now that I am out of there, I will keep my vows.' And in verse 13, he says "you have delivered my soul from death". How truthful is it! He should have been killed by the sword by the Philistine King but God protected him.

The second Psalm he wrote was Psalm 34. The heading of that Psalm tells us explicitly that he wrote it immediately after he escaped from King, Achesh. This is what we read in verse 4, "he delivered me from all my fears". In verse he says, "He saved me out of all my troubles" and in verse 11 he says "because I went through all of this, I have something to teach the rest of you". He says "I will teach the ways of the Lord." David is telling us not to make the mistake that he made.

When things don't go the way you expect and you go through a tough time in your life, put your trust in God, and completely trust in God. Even when it doesn't even make any sense, put your trust in Him. And if you're going to fear anyone, fear only God. Don't fear man; don't allow the fear of man take over your life. Because the Bible teaches the fear of man is a trap. If you allow the fear of man to take over your life, it can become dysfunctional. It can destroy your life. You can end up as a psychiatric patient. Do not allow fear to take over your life, trust in God.

Let us look again at the stone that we came across in 1Samuel, chapter 20. Do you know that we have also come to a stone? There is a stone in our lives also. In Daniel 2:4, this is a stone that is cut out without hands. Daniel said at the end of that dream to Nebuchadnezzar, in history there will come a stone that is not cut out by the hands of man. He was talking about the kingdom of Jesus Christ. The Bible tells us, he came not by the will of man. And therefore he is a stone cut without hands.

In Isaiah, chapter 28, verse 16, the Bible tells us he is a precious cornerstone. When we believe in Jesus Christ, he becomes the cornerstone of our life. The Bible says that it is an immovable stone. In 1Peter 2:4, Peter tells us that he is a true and living stone. And come to this living stone so that you can be transformed by him. In 1Peter2:7, this is the stone that the builders rejected but has become the cornerstone of the house. And who is that stone? We know that stone is Jesus Christ, the rock of ages. And that is why Isaiah 28 tells of Him that he is a sure foundation. If you are going through a tough season in your life, come to the sure foundation. Everything else is nothing but sinking stand. Come to the rock of ages.

If you put your trust in Him, He will see you through this tough season in your life. It will not last. There are tremendous blessings from God waiting for you.

The promises in the life of David were eventually fulfilled. David did become the King, he did get the throne. But when you through that very tough time in your life it is very difficult to look beyond the immediate realities of your life and think about the promises. The one who gave you the promises is a faithful God. What a friend we have in Jesus!

Chapter VII

Outside the Camp

When David reached Adullam, he realized that it was the refuge God had prepared for him for that season in his life. God will never leave His children without a refuge. His ways are higher than our ways and His thoughts are higher than our thoughts. So we are better off trusting in Him than trying to figure out things on our own. Just as saw in the life of David, when we try to do that, we make a fool of ourselves.

Nonetheless, David is alone now and he thinks the whole world has forgotten about him. No one remembers what he did for the nation; no one remembers the great victory he had over Goliath—at least that he thinks. But when we read through 1 Samuel, chapter 22, we see that things unfolded in a different way.

> "David therefore departed from there and escaped to the cave of Adullam. So when his brothers and all his father's house heard [it], they went down there to him. And everyone [who was] in distress, everyone who [was] in debt, and everyone [who was] discontented gathered to him. So he became captain over them. And there were about four hundred men with him." (1 Samuel 22:1, 2).

Immediately David had a following of about four hundred people. When you are a leader, you will always have a group of people to follow you. God will see to it. As long as you are in God's will, things will fall in place. But when you look at the people, they were 'everyone who was in distress, everyone who was in debt, and everyone who was discontented. This was not the palace crowd.

This was a training period in the life of David and God wanted him to work with these people and turn them into a mighty army. In that process, he would develop and prove his leadership skills.

But when David was running around confused, no one joined with him or came to his rescue. He still had the anointing. But he was not settled in God's will for that season. God cannot use you until you are settled in God's will. You are created to be a blessing to yourself and others. But no one will get anything out of your life until you are settled in God's will.

Once you are, God will move things on your behalf. People started coming to David. He had nothing to offer them. He was living in a cave. It did not matter. They came and identified with his call. So stop fighting with God. Believe that God is control of your life today and allow Him to move in your life. You may think that you have nothing to offer to others. But people can see the fingerprints of God in your life. They sense the presence of God in your life. They will gravitate toward you. All you have to do is to settle down and be at peace.

When David had victory over Goliath, people saw that he had military genius and the ability to think outside the box. But he was not a leader of men. Now God is sending needy people in his life to train him by taking care of them and creating a bond with others. It was hands on leadership training.

God was doing him a favor. King Saul had issues because he had no raining in becoming a leader. One day he was looking for the donkeys of his father and he was anointed as king. No wonder people found him walking after the donkeys even after his impromptu coronation. He was never ready to be a king. Saul never learned the art of leading men and messed up as a leader. God did not want David to make the same mistake.

God was allowing David to progress step by step. Before he was given the whole nation, he was given a band of four hundred people.

God always test us out with small assignments. If we are found faithful in little things, then we are given much. So if you are team leader with just five people in your team, do not fuss about it. You may feel like 'I can handle a lot more than this. Why am I given such a small task?' Many times people react like the man who was just given one talent. He did not want to bother. It is a training season in your life. Do your job faithfully. God will take you to greater heights later.

During this season in the life of David, we can see many parallels between Jesus and David. First of all, we see David was anointed to be king, while someone else was sitting on the throne. God has already declared that He has set His king in Zion (Psalm 2:6). Jesus is already declared king of this earth while Satan is ruling it.

Secondly, Saul does his best to stop David from assuming the throne. The same way Satan tried his best to finish off Jesus before he could be declared the king. Starting from Abraham, we see that many of the wives of the patriarchs were barren. Their husbands had to wait prayerfully for years to see a child. Sarah, Rebecca and Rachel were barren for three generations in a row. It was an attempt to cut off the seed line. Satan knew that the 'seed of the woman will come and crush the head of the serpent.' When it did not work, he corrupted the entire nation of Israel many times hoping that God would give up on them and the seed line would be cut off. Later, David was promised a son in every generation so that the lineage of Messiah would continue. But the lineage was almost cut off when the last king died without a son. After baby Jesus was born, Herod decreed to kill all the male children under two hoping to kill Jesus in that process. When Jesus started his public ministry, Satan tempted him three times hoping to divert him from his mission. When he crucified, Satan thought he had stopped Jesus from becoming the king. But when he resurrected, all authority was given to him and he is already declared as the king of the earth.

Thirdly, David was anointed as the future king among his brothers. He was given a grand stage on the day he had victory over Goliath. He had a royal introduction that day. People were singing in the streets about David. But then he was 'sent away' by God for his time to become king had not come. The same way, Jesus was declared as the 'King of the Jews' and 'the savior of the world' at his birth. The angels came down to announce his birth. The king on the throne came to know about him. Jesus was introduced to the pious at the temple as a baby. He was introduced to the Jewish scholars at the age of twelve. He was known by multiple thousands during his public ministry. More than once, God declared, 'This is my beloved Son. Listen to him.' On Palm Sunday, the streets of Jerusalem were filled with people carrying palm leaves and singing Hosanna to Jesus. But then he went through the passion experience and has gone to heaven, away from the people he came to save, for a while. He is asked to "Sit at My right hand, till I make your enemies your footstool." (Psalm 110:1)

Fourthly, despite wasting all the resources of the kingdom, Saul could never stop David. The same is true about Christianity, the body of Jesus on earth. Starting in Acts, chapter 3, authorities tried to snuff out the nascent church in its infancy. Jewish authorities could not do it. Herod did not succeed in it. The ten waves of persecution unleashed against Christians by Romans during the first three centuries of the Common Era, did not succeed in wiping out Christianity. All the 'cleaning' by communists did not do that in the twentieth century. His church is still marching on! The end time persecution yet to come will not succeed either. Diluting the church doctrines or the unbelievable liberalism in main line churches will not stop Christianity either. God will always have his remnant to work with.

Fifthly, when the time came, God moved in history to remove Saul from the stage and allowed David to assume the throne that was promised him a long time ago. The same way, god is still in control of history and he will move the pieces of history when His time comes to prepare the way for Jesus to come and take over the rulership of this world. He has already foretold how it will unfold in Daniel 2, 7, Mathew 24; Revelation, chapters 5 to 21 etc.

If you look at the people who came and joined with David, again you can see a parallel to the people who have joined with Christ. There are five things that we can note about them.

First of all, we see that these are people seeking refuge. These were people in distress or people with various issues in life. Some were in debt or facing bankruptcy and were escaping the strong arm of the law when they came to David. Though Jesus will never condone that, so many people in debt have come to Jesus and had their prayers answered. The third group of people was 'discontented,' people who had no satisfaction in life, people who were finding it difficult to see any meaning for life. People who were searching for a reason to live. How true is that about millions of people who follow Jesus today!

This is what Bible tells about us: "by two immutable things, in which it is impossible for God to lie, we might have strong consolation, who have fled for refuge to lay hold of the hope set before us." (Hebrews 6:18). We are a group of people who have fled the kingdom of Satan and sought refuge in Jesus. Whatever God has promised to that group is immutable. It will not change.

Secondly, the Bible introduces David as their 'captain.' David became the captain of people whom no one else wanted. Jesus is called the 'captain of our salvation.' (Hebrews 2:10). He has promised 'the one who comes to **Me** I will by no means cast out.' (John 6:37). He is not ashamed of the people who are distressed, who are in debt and who are discontented.

Within Christianity we have crystal cathedrals and multimillion dollar ultra modern sanctuaries and also congregations that worship the same Jesus under a tree or in a small thatched hut. Social standing is not an issue in worshipping God.

Jesus has already shown in history that he meant every promise he gave. When he was on earth he went after the people whom no one else wanted—the lepers, the blind, the homeless, the prostitutes, the demon possessed and the publicans. Many times he went out of his way to meet them. One night he weathered the storm and put the lives of his followers in jeopardy to seek after one demon possessed young man. When society wanted to criticize them for coming to Jesus, he would always defend them. Jesus still wants the people whom no one cares for. That is why Christianity is so deep in charitable works.

Thirdly, David shaped the destiny of the people who came to him. They started out as a rag tag army. But they came to be known as the 'mighty men of David' later. (1 Chronicles 11:10). The same way Jesus moulds us when we come to him. Jeremiah gives us the beautiful picture of the potter and the clay. Just as a potter take a lump of clay and make a vessel that he has already pictured in his mind, God will take us who are taken from the earth and will mould us until we fit perfectly in His hands.

Peter uses another language to tell us about this process. "Coming to Him as to a living stone, rejected indeed by men, but chosen by God and precious, you also, as living stones, are being built up a spiritual house, a holy priesthood, to offer up spiritual sacrifices acceptable to God through Jesus Christ." (1 Peter 2:4, 5). We come to Jesus with our stony hearts. He works on us and transforms us and we become a beautiful edifice for the glory of God.

Fourthly, we cannot but marvel at the glory of the end product. The motley crew that joined with David was continuously improved. Seeing that more people joined with him. People from every tribe in Israel came to David eventually—even from the tribe of Benjamin, the tribe of King Saul. 1 Chronicles 12 gives a list of all the people who came to David at Ziklag. They are described as, **mighty men of valor, men** trained for battle, who could handle shield and spear, whose faces [were like] the faces **of** lions, and [were] as swift as gazelles on the mountains:' (1 Chronicles 12:8).

The same thing has happened to Christianity. Initially it was just the humble folks who followed Jesus. But after witnessing how Jesus transforms and blesses everyone who follows him, people from all walks of life started joining the ranks. Today we will see multimillionaires and hourly workers sitting next to each other and worshipping Jesus in the same church. In our church we have fourteen different nationalities. One church I know in New York City has people from ninety eight different nations!

Where else can see such harmony? I know that the eastern gurus try to practice that when they come to the west as a marketing ploy. But go their nations and see the discrimination against others based on caste, education level, financial status etc.

The message of Christianity is the most glorious message ever given to mankind: to break down the partitions that held us separate and to unite at the foot of the cross as partakers of one bread.

We also see that the enemy of David hated anyone who had anything to do with David also. Saul had no qualm in killing eighty five members of priestly families just for giving bread to David. He tried to kill his own son Jonathan for supporting David. Isn't it the same story about Christianity?

I was born and brought up in the nation of India. The majority Hindus are a very peaceful people generally. But when the fanatic gurus (it is always the gurus who whip up the emotions of the people), instigate them, something happens. They become ghoulish. I cannot still fathom how a peaceful people can transform into murderers who will douse a jeep with gasoline and burn to death a father and two sons who were just sleeping at a rest stop, just because they are Christians. I do not know how can such nice people can become rapists of nuns without any sense of shame and ask them to march down the street naked. How can they raze entire villages and drive thousands of people into deep forests just for being Christians? Where does such deep hatred come from? I refuse to believe it is not human. I have more confidence in my fellow human beings.

But when the spirit of the one who hated Jesus all along gets into someone they are filled with rage and hatred. The spirit of murder that manifested in Cain continues to rage against their brothers who simply live in obedience to the word of God to this day.

David told his followers, "Stay with me; do not fear. For he who seeks my life seeks your life, but with me you shall be safe." (1 Samuel 22:23). None of the people who joined with David was lost. The same way, Jesus told his followers that the world will despise them. But he promised, 'lo, I am with you always, even to the end of the age.' (Mathew 28:20)

CHAPTER VIII

In The School of Adversity

We are still meditating on the life of David during the time he was sent away from the palace. We saw that it was a very difficult time in his life. When he came to Adullam, he realized it was the safe haven for him for a while and once he was settled people started coming to him. It shows that our ministry cannot take off until we are settled in our personal lives.

In this chapter, we will start our meditation in 1 Samuel 22. We see that once we are settled in God's will, He will make provisions for us and assumes the re3sponsibility of our welfare. In the case of David, we see that God sent a prophet named Gad to him. Now he can hear God's voice again. Remember what he told the king of Moab earlier, "until I find out what God will do for me.' For a period he did not hear from the Lord and it was driving David crazy. We saw the crazy unexpected side steps in his life. This was a very capable man on many fronts. But he desperately needed counsel from God and godly friends. On other occasions, David did some unexpected things. Now that Gad is here, he can hear the godly counsel again.

Later on, God also sent the priest Abiathar to David. He brought with him the ephod. On ephod w2as the plates called Urim and Tummim which the people of Israel used to get answers from the Lord. By sending Abiathar to him, God was telling David that He was ready to give him answers. For a while David only had questions. Now God is ready to giv3 him answers. Thus we can see that God will not leave us alone for a long time without a means to hear from him. The Holy Spirit living in us will make sure of that.

All of these pieces started falling in place once David was settled in his personal life and was ready to surrender to God's will for that season in his life. David is still in a cave. But the presence of God is with him. A child of God cherishes God's presence more than the luxuries of the world. That is the assurance that God is still with us.

In 1 Samuel 23, we see the phrase 'David enquired of the Lord' is repeated many times. It was possible because of the presence of ephod. Worship is restored in the life of this child of God.

In that chapter, we also get to see the David's heart again. Here he is a fugitive from the king's army. But when he heard that the Philistines came and attacked the border town of Keilah, he immediately went to fight them. He did not say, 'since the nation does not want me, let them suffer.' This was still his people and he was going to be their king one day despite the current set back. So he went out of his way to protect Israel. No wonder God declared that David had his heart in the right place.

David's men were not crazy about the idea. But David's men said to him, "Look, we are afraid here in Judah. How much more then if we go to Keilah against the armies of the Philistines?" (1 Samuel 23:2). Don't you know they are looking for us? Why are you exposing us to both the armies of King Saul and the Philistines? But David inquired of the Lord and He said go. That is all that mattered to David. His confidence is back! He is trusting in God again to take care of him and his men!

A child of God is not motivated by the reward. We do things because the love of Christ compels us. It is up to God to decide how to reward us. It is impossible for a child of God to stay on the sideline, even when danger is foreseen. Also, a child of God has to do what is required of him or she even when it looks like nobody appreciates them.

That is the problem with calling. The call wakes you up to commitment. When others shrug off, you cannot. Jeremiah understood that. He was called into prophetic ministry by God at a very young age. But people did not appreciate his ministry. He was harassed, jailed; his legs were placed in wooden locks and even half drowned in a sand pit. Finally he decided not to speak in God's name anymore. But the call upon his life would not leave him alone. This is the way tells us of that experience:

Then I said, "I will not make mention of Him, Nor speak anymore in His name." But [His word] was in my heart like a burning fire Shut up in my bones; I was weary of holding [it] back, And I could not." (Jeremiah 20:9). No wonder God said, 'Who is a fool like My servant?' The next time if you see your minister doing something crazy like committing to help others when you have no money, please understand their heart.

So David went and defended the city of Keilah from the hands of Philistines. But as the war was winding down, David began to feel that these people instead of being grateful to him and his men forever would actually betray them. As a border town, they dependent on the 'federal budget' of Saul. They could get a huge bounty for David. So they were ready to cash him in.

David probably had other plans. Keilah was a border town, away from the palace of Saul. Secondly it was a walled city. Here they were living in caves for a while. Naturally an opportunity to live in a walled city would be a welcome change. So if David thought in gratitude for saving them from Philistines, the people of Keilah would welcome him and his militia to stay with them, can we blame him? That may be the reason for him to come out of the safety of Adullam and expose himself and his men.

But true to human nature, the folks in Keilah turned their back on David. Their behavior was less than welcoming, as if David was imposing himself on them. So he inquired of the Lord and the answer was they would hand him over to Saul. So here was David running again. Trying to show the love for his people, he found himself a wanderer again.

But this time there was a big difference in David. He was not going crazy like before. There was a peace in his life. It was because the worship was restored in his life and presence of God was with him. That is what the Bible promises us. The peace of God passes all understanding. Despite the situation in your life, the God of peace can keep your thoughts and imaginations under check.

When you are a child of God, what really matters is not conditions in which you find yourself, it is the condition of your heart. Do you have peace in your heart? Jesus is the prince of peace. He promised to give us his peace. He said it is not like the peace the world gives. The peace the world gives is conditional. Conditions are in your favor and you have peace. But the peace that Jesus gives is peace in the midst of adversity. Do we have that kind of peace in us?

David became a wanderer looking for a hiding place. He went to a number of cities but they all wanted to hand him over to Saul. When we come to the end of 1 Samuel, chapter 23, Saul is in pursuit of David in person. Saul had vowed not to rest until he kill the son of Jesse. But we see divine protection on the life of David. Saul and his army would be on one side of the mountain and David and his men would be on the other side of the mountain. Still there is peace in the life of David as he is settled in the will of God. While you are in a school of adversity, if your heart is not settled, it will become unbearable.

Then King Saul got smarter and divided his army into two hoping to corner David. Surely David would have been cornered if God had not intervened. All of a sudden Saul heard that another nation is attacking Israel and he was forced to go back to his palace. God knows how to take care of His own! His ways are higher than our ways. He knows how to defend and protect His people. It took no input from David, it was totally God. God will make a way, where there is no way. When the enemy thinks he has you surrounded, God provides a way out for you. Even if He has to split open a sea, He will do it. No wonder David said, 'though an army encamps around me, I will not fear. He will protect me in His pavilion.' We do not know how it is going to work out, but it will work out. No weapon fashioned against you will prosper.

Saul came back though. In an earlier chapter we saw how a murderous spirit got in Saul which prompted him to go after David. Eventually David ended up in a very rugged area called En Gedi. The word means 'young goat.' The area was so rugged that it had become the play ground of ibex. The elderly Saul followed David into the En Gedi area, climbing the lime stone mountains. "I will look for him throughout all the clans of Judah,' Saul said. (1 Samuel 23:23). Look at the power of hatred!

While Saul who lost the anointing was propelled by hatred, we see how a man who carries the anointing behaves in the response of David. In 1 Samuel 24 and 26 we see two incidents where David spared the life of Saul.

Saul would be looking for David in the heat of the day and after a while he would tired and want to rest. The only place with shade in that part of the world is the caves. So Saul would creep into a big cave seeking rest. One time it was the same cave where David and his men were hiding deep inside. David's men went to him and said, "This is the day of which the Lord said to you, 'behold, I will deliver your enemy into your hands that you may do to him as it seem good to you.'" (1 Samuel 24:4). God said no such thing. It sounded like a prophecy. But it was not true.

David's men knew he would listen to a word from the Lord. So they gave their opinion a religious color. There is a big difference between religious spirit and the Holy Spirit.

It is easy to understand the frustration of the people of David. Saul was chasing them all over En Gedi. If it was not for the intervention of God, none of them would be alive that day. Now, here is their arch enemy delivered into their hands. Why not look it as a divine providence? Why not finish him off so they can stop running? So the men of David screamed in his ears, "This is God. This is God. Look what God has done for us. Arise and finish him off in the name of the Lord."

But David would not. He knew it was not God. What prompted Saul to run after David at an elderly age was not God; it was a murderous spirit from Satan.

A true child of God is always careful not to mix the two and discern things. It was the inability to do this during the Middle Ages that led to the Crusades and bloodshed in the name of religion. It is a black spot on Christianity to this day. Religion can be misused for personal gain and we can good examples of that here. Every time someone came to Saul and said David is hiding at a particular place, he would say, "The Lord has put me in my hands. Today the Lord will let me get him. The Lord will be with me." When Saul ended up in the same cave where David and his men were, David's men said, "The Lord has put Saul in our hands." Both sides quoting the Lord while both are outside the will of God! Everyone says, 'Thus says the Lord' while the Lord has not spoken to any of them.

David crept up to the spot where Saul was sleeping and cut off the edge of his garment, for proof that David could have done more. David began to feel guilty about even that. When Saul woke up and left the cave, David cried out after a few minutes about what happened and asked Saul to look at his clothes for proof. When Saul realized the truth, he wept bitterly and said, "You are more righteous than I." Then Saul went back to his palace.

But he came back though. When Ziphites went to Saul and pointed out where David was hiding, he could not pass up that chance. So Saul found himself in the mountains of En Gedi again.

The story in 1Samuel 26 is similar to the one in chapter 24. This time Saul and his men were sleeping outside one night. David and one of his generals, Abishai, crept up to him again among the sleeping soldiers. Again the general said, Then Abishai said to David, "God has delivered your enemy into your hand this day. Now therefore, please, let me strike him at once with the spear, right to the earth; and I will not [have to strike] him a second time!" (! Samuel 26:8). But David said, "Do not destroy him; for who can stretch out his hand against the LORD's anointed, and be guiltless? The LORD forbid that I should stretch out my hand against the LORD's anointed." (1 Samuel 26:9, 11).

There is a tremendous spiritual lesson here. All of us make comments about other ministers, like we know them, we know what they went through in their lives, how they think, what propels them etc. People jab ministers with impunity. It is not really our job. David's attitude is the best: 'Let God take care of him. I will not touch God's anointed.'

He took the pitcher from which Saul drank and went back to a distance and shouted," "Why does my lord thus pursue his servant? For what have I done, or what evil [is] in my hand?" (1

73

Samuel 26:18). David pointed to the pitcher and the spear he took from Saul.

When Saul realized that David had spared his life a second time, he came to his senses and said, "Then Saul said, "I have sinned. Return, my son David. For I will harm you no more, because my life was precious in your eyes this day. Indeed I have played the fool and erred exceedingly." (1 Samuel 26:21).

The story ends in an unusual way. The man who came to kill David ended up blessing him. Saul could see that David was much more righteous than him. He could see that David was much more king material than him. So he blessed David and said, ""May you be blessed, my son David! You shall both do great things and also still prevail." (1 Samuel 26:25).

When your heart is in the right place, everything else will follow. You may be in the school of adversity right now. But guard your heart. It is easy become bitter and take things into one's own hands. It is easy to compromise and say the Lord has given me this opportunity and I will use it. It is easy to take revenge on people and thank God for the opportunity. Beware! Guard your heart! Trust in the Lord completely. In all your actions remember that God will never violate the principles He has established in His word. Stick to His word. He will take care of everything.

Imagine what can happen when you remain faithful. The enemies who want to finish you off will end up blessing you seeing the godliness in you.

There are three Psalms that David wrote during this time that also gives us a glimpse into his godly heart. They are Psalms 27, 31 and 54. In Psalm 27 David wrote: "Though an army may encamp against me, My heart shall not fear; Though war may rise against me, In this I [will be] confident." (v.3). "For in the time of trouble He shall hide me in His pavilion; In the secret place of His tabernacle He shall hide me; He shall set me high upon a rock." (v.5). He also tells what happens when we trust in the Lord. "And now my head shall be lifted up above my enemies all around me; Therefore I will offer sacrifices of joy in His tabernacle; I will sing, yes, I will sing praises to the LORD." (v.6). If you wonder how David could act that way, the secret is given to us in verse 8. He heard the Lord's voice, "Seek My face." That is the same advice given to us today. "For consider Him who endured such hostility from sinners against Himself, lest you become weary and discouraged in your souls." (Hebrews 12:3).

What was David's response when the people of Keilah betrayed him? "I am forgotten like a dead man, out of mind; I am like a broken vessel. For I hear the slander of many; Fear [is] on every side; While they take counsel together against me, They scheme to take away my life. But as for me, I trust in You, O LORD; I say, "You [are] my God." My times [are] in Your hand." (Psalm 31:12-15). David could see he was 'like a dead man forgotten by men.' The only time someone was talking about him was when they were slandering him. No one said one good word about him. It did not matter since 'my times are in Your hand.' No one would control his destiny, but God. They could slander all they wanted. They could mistreat him unfairly. He would go through tough times. But Him times were in God's hand.

He had confidence. "You shall hide them in the secret place of Your presence from the plots of man; You shall keep them secretly in a pavilion from the strife of tongues." (v.20). David has a word for you today. "Oh, love the LORD, all you His saints! [For] the LORD preserves the faithful, And fully repays the proud person. Be of good courage, And He shall strengthen your heart, All you who hope in the LORD." (v.23, 24).

Even Jesus had to go through the school of adversity. In the garden of Gethsemane, he cried out under the burden of it, 'Remove this cup from me.' But as kept seeking the will of his Father, he realized that he must endure it for the glory to follow. So he surrendered himself and said, 'Not my will, let Thy will be done.' He is our example in the school of adversity. We must look at him when we need answers lest we become wearied.

Wallace Harley was a band master in England. He grew up in a Methodist church in England. His father was the choir master in that church. 'Nearer my Lord to thee' was his father's favorite song. Wallace grew up hearing that song and he loved it. He used to tell other s that that is the song he wanted played at the time of his funeral. Later he became the band master of RMS Titanic. When the ship started sinking, there was bedlam on board. People were clinging to whatever they could find. Knowing that things are not playing out the way he expected, Wallace decided to play for others the song that he wanted to be played for him. As the ship went under, the band kept playing, 'Nearer My God to thee.' Wallace was not delivered from death that day. But nonetheless he chose to trust in God, knowing that even then, his soul is secure for eternity in the Lord.

Can you trust God when you are going through tough times?

CHAPTER IX

What Does Your Heart Say?

The single most important thing in the life of children of God is the promises upon their lives. We build our lives based on it. Many of us are waiting for many of the promises to be fulfilled in our lives. The most difficult season in our lives is this waiting period. Somehow you must the courage to hold on till that day. But we realize that there is an enemy bent on making sure that we do not get to walk in our promises.

That is where David was. Here he is struggling to hold on, struggling to keep the restless followers on line, keeping the testosterone in check. But then his enemy, King Saul, made it so hard for him by chasing him and his people around. On top of that David had made up his mind that he would not touch the anointed of God. If he did not want to do it, others were willing to do it for him. But he would not allow anyone to touch Saul. The people were struggling under pressure.

We will take a closer look at that time period in this chapter. We will be looking at 1 Samuel, chapters 25 to 30 for this lesson. The struggles of that time period can be summarized in what we see in 1 Samuel 27:1. "And David said in his heart, "Now I shall perish someday by the hand of Saul. [There is] nothing better for me than that I should speedily escape to the land of the Philistines; and Saul will despair of me, to seek me anymore in any part of Israel. So I shall escape out of his hand."

Initially when God thrust him into this phase of his life, he was totally confused and made many wrong decisions that caused harm to him and others. When he reached Adullam and settled down in God's will, God had started sending people to him so that he can emerge later as a people's leader. We saw earlier that after prophet Gad and priest Abiathar joined with him, David had a positive outlook on things for a while. He was also enjoying God's protection during that time. Despite all the attempts of King Saul, despite multiple betrayals by many he trusted, the enemy could not touch him.

But as time dragged on, and Saul was relentless in his pursuit of David, David heart began to sink again. It is only natural to feel that way. Time can break down the strongest among us. 'David said in his heart' it is not happening, as many of us do, when we get tired of waiting. We saw his admonition to us when there was hope in his heart. "Be of good courage, And He shall strengthen your heart, All you who hope in the LORD." (Psalm 31:24). The man who asked us to strengthen our hearts by trusting in God is weakened in his heart by the delay.

What happened? By the time we come to 1 Samuel, chapter 25, David has an established militia and six hundred families are depending on him. They were primarily a mercenary group that would give protection for the border towns of Israel and the farmers living there. In return they would feed David and the people who were with him. In chapter we see a very rich farmer named Nabal whom David's militia had protected in the past. He was having a shearing festival. It was commonplace to feed the feed at such festive occasions. David sent his men to Nabal hoping that they would invite them also for the festival. He reminded his services to him.

"Now I have heard that you have shearers. Your shepherds were with us, and we did not hurt them, nor was there anything missing from them all the while they were in Carmel. 'Ask your young men, and they will tell you. Therefore let [my] young men find favor in your eyes, for we come on a feast day. Please give whatever comes to your hand to your servants and to your son David." (1 Samuel 25:7, 8).

The reply from Nabal was totally unexpected. 'Then Nabal answered David's servants, and said, "Who is David, and who is the son of Jesse? There are many servants nowadays who break away each one from his master. Shall I then take my bread and my water and my meat that I have killed for my shearers, and give it to men when I do not know where they [are] from?"' (1 Samuel 25:10, 11).

David was shocked. Everywhere he turned, despite his good heart, despite his willingness to help others, people were negative to him. It should have perplexed David immensely. Most of the people were looking at David as a person trying to snatch the throne from Saul's family. David got tired of explain to people how Samuel came to his home and anointed him when even his own family did not consider him worthy of the anointing. It looked like no one was buying it. The general impression was David was a warrior in the army of Saul who became a rebel leader trying to oust the king.

Please remember that just because you are anointed, everyone will accept you. When you are used in a church or in a ministry setting, people may look at you as someone usurping and trying to become a leader. You may be even accused of even trying to replace the existing leader.

This can happen in your work place also. When people begin to see you are talented and you have potential, many will begin to look at you as an enemy to be quelled, rather than joining the choir singing your praises.

Nabal was a very rich man whose shepherds had enjoyed the protection David's mercenary provided. But when the time came to recognize him publicly, Nabal retorted, 'Who is David?'

This is a situation young ministers face very often. The Holy Spirit will give them messages and ideas and they serve free of charge anyone who is willing to use them. But many times, when it is time to recognize them, the same institutions and ministers will turn around and act like they do not know them. Very few people come forward to help others to reach their destiny. Those whom they help may far exceed them and may be a greater help to the helpers in the future. But very few people see it.

The message from David was this: 'You know the anointing upon me and where I am going. If you help me a little during this waiting period in my life, I will never forget you and will be a greater help to you when I get there.' Nabal did not see it. No wonder his wife sent word to David that her husband is a foolish man.

One day a Caucasian Pastor visited our church in New York and told us this incident. His church is in a small town in Indiana. Some years ago, an African American pastor of a small store front church in West Virginia tried to befriend him. He called him and asked him to accommodate a pastor that was a blessing to his church in West Virginia. He said if he had done that, they would have become friends. But he turned him down saying, 'Who is this guy to use a minister whom he recommends?' How far can a pastor of a store front church go? He never heard from that pastor again. That pastor was Bishop T.D. Jakes!

Be on the lookout for the people on their way up. Do whatever you can to help them get there. When they get here, they will not forget you. Do not be fools like Nabal.

Even Jesus said, if you give a glass of water to someone, you will get a reward. Sometimes all you do is say an encouraging word. It cost you nothing. But the reward may be amazing.

Nabal really got under the skin of David. He gathered his soldiers and was on his way to kill Nabal and take his flocks altogether, when his wife met him and handles the situation wisely. Had David done that, it would have ruined his godly testimony. He would have become just another strong arm militia leader. Others can get under your skin. But you cannot forget even then that you are a child of God. His future would have been tainted. God used Nabal's wise wife Abigail to stop David from committing that atrocity. Her message was, 'Nabal may be refusing to give you food today. Do not let him control your destiny tomorrow. Don't let this fool stop you from being all God want you to be—a godly king on the throne.' David realized his mistake and thanked God for stopping him in time.

Abigail is a picture of Holy Spirit. How many times Holy Spirit stopped us from tainting our testimonies? Many times we just want to let loose and let them have it. But Holy Spirit always stops us. Always seek the help of the Holy Spirit when people get under your skin.

In 1 Samuel 27, we see David sinking into depression. The first verse of that chapter is a classical statement of a depressed person. There are many who believe that if you are a child of God, you cannot go through depression. All you have to do is to cast out the spirit of depression. That is foolishness.

I know many Christians who have suffered from depression and had to seek medical treatment. We are all humans. When things do not go the way we expect it to, there will be tension in our lives. Once that tension reaches a certain stage and nothing changes, something has to give way. Our minds may give up under the relentless pressure. Sometimes Satan does a water boarding of your mind.

This was not the only occasion in David's life when he felt that way. In Psalm 10, verse 1, he cried out, "Why do You stand afar off, O LORD? Why do You hide in times of trouble?" In Psalm 13, verse 1and 2, he cried, "How long, O LORD? Will You forget me forever? How long will You hide Your face from me? How long shall I take counsel in my soul, Having sorrow in my heart daily? How long will my enemy be exalted over me? "Psalm 22, verses 1 and 2, is another expression of how he felt. "My God, My God, why have You forsaken Me? Why are You so far from helping Me, And from the words of My groaning? O My God, I cry in the daytime, but You do not hear; And in the night season, and am not silent."

It is natural to feel this way. But our thoughts have consequences. When we dwell on negative thoughts always, it opens a door for the enemy to enter into our mind and lead us away from the plans of God. In 1 Samuel 27, when the David's heart was sending him the negative messages, he once again took some bad decisions. (By now, you can see that despite being a godly person, David did not fare very well under pressure).

He had two enemy fronts he had to face. On one side was King Saul who was hell bent on destroying him. On the other side were the Philistines, the arch enemy of Israel. The only bargain chip David had was his militia. So he decided to go to Philistines and offer his services for hire to survive. But it was giving into the enemy. He decided to enter into a covenant with the arch enemy of the people of God. He decided there was point in holding on anymore.

But the enemy does not celebrate you. He does not care who you are, what your destiny is or when or whether you will get there. If you join with him, he will just use you as a slave as long as long as he can. That is what happened to David when he went to the Philistines.

"Then David arose and went over with the six hundred men who [were] with him to Achish the son of Maoch, king of Gath. So David dwelt with Achish at Gath, he and his men, each man with his household, [and] David with his two wives, Ahinoam the Jezreelitess, and Abigail the Carmelitess, Nabal's widow." (1 Samuel 27:2, 3)

David thought he had immigrated to another country. He has his family with him. His men have their family with them. This is it! Especially, now that Saul is no longer looking for him. Just be mercenaries to Achish and survive. The king gave them a place called Ziklag and they settled down there.

David started acting like he completely forgot his destiny. He and his men started acting like thugs, raiding communities and wiping out entire communities. When the king asked him about the raids, he would lie through his teeth. Achish believed that he got a lifelong slave. 'So Achish believed David, saying, "He has made his people Israel utterly abhor him; therefore he will be my servant forever."' (1 Samuel 27:12). Achish reported, "And to this day I have found no fault in him since he defected to me." (1 Samuel 29:3).

Things changed when Achish and the Philistines decided to attack Israel. Now David was forced to go against his own people. He could not say no. God had to move in the heart of the nobles of Philistines to save David's face that day. The troubles we put God through sometimes!

Realities of life have a great gravitational pull. David had six hundred families to feed. He thought he had no choice but to compromise to survive. I have heard about young ladies intentionally going into sex trade thinking that is the only way to survive. It always shocks me. Because history is full of examples that they are walking into a trap from which most people never come out.

What is your heart telling you today? You may be tired of waiting. You may be considering to compromise. Do not! As Habakkuk said, 'Wait for it. Even if it tarries, it will come.' "For the vision is yet for an appointed time; But at the end it will speak, and it will not lie. Though it tarries, wait for it; because it will surely come, it will not tarry." (Hab. 2:3).

Your lies will eventually catch with you. Ask anyone in history. You may live a life of lies and act perfect for a while. But the day of reckoning will come. It came to David on two fronts. First, the nobles among Philistines confronted him and king who blindly believed him. They told the king to send David back to Ziklag. They were sure that the David was putting up a show and that in a battle against Israel; he would never attack his own people.

David and his men had mercilessly attacked the nomadic tribe of Amalekites again and aging and plundered them. He wiped out many of their communities. So they were waiting for an opportunity. When they heard that David and his man had gone with the Philistines, they got their opportunity.

> "Now it happened, when David and his men came to Ziklag, on the third day, that the Amalekites had invaded the South and Ziklag, attacked Ziklag and burned it with fire, and had taken captive the women and those who were there, from small to great; they did not kill anyone, but carried them away and went their way." (1 Samuel 30:1, 2).

Even though it was horrible, they were more righteous than David. They only took the people captive. They did not wipe them out.

But that was no solace for the men who were with David. They had it with him. They were putting up with him reluctantly for a long time. They were all tired of waiting for God's time. All they had was their family members and a few cattle. Now that even that was taken from them, they turned against David. 'The people spoke of stoning him, because the soul of all the people was grieved, every man for his sons and his daughters.' (1 Samuel 30:6).

The Amalekites would not have attacked David's camp, if he had not plundered them so many times. You will always reap based on what you sow. If we compromise for the moment's sake, there is a big harvest of destruction coming in the future.

David was looking around for a way out. He saw the people were ready to stone him. He needed answers fast. That is when he realized the ephod was right there. Knowing that he can get an answer from the Lord, he strengthened himself. Had he asked for God's guidance this tragedy could have been avoided. Then he would have never gone to the Philistines.

Once his focus turned to God, things began to fall in place again. He asked of the Lord and He gave him direction. Following that direction, he pursued the Amalekites and killed them and recovered everything. "So David recovered all that the Amalekites had carried away, and David rescued his two wives. And nothing of theirs was lacking, either small or great, sons or daughters, spoil or anything which they had taken from them; David recovered all." (1 Samuel 30:18, 19).

What is your heart saying today? Your heart should not be your ultimate guide. It must be the word of God and God's promises in your life. Even when things looks bleak and everything within you scream to compromise, do not. Otherwise you will have a lot of bracket periods and unwanted additions to your life story. Hold on to God's promises. The one who gave you the promises is faithful. He will fulfill them.

CHAPTER X

Transition Trials

We have been focusing on the interim time period in the life of David for a few chapters. We learned a number of principles from there that we can use in our day to day lives. Now we have come to the next stage in his life. The waiting period is over. And God is in the process of establishing what was promised into his life a long time ago.

God had removed Saul from the stage. David had taken a stand that he would not touch God's anointed. He committed to wait until God dealt with Saul. Finally Saul and his son Jonathan were killed in another battle with Philistines. That was the battle into which the Philistine king had originally invited David, who was their hired mercenary at that time. He almost messed up everything. Imagine David fighting with Philistines against the Israel and coming a few months later wanting to become the king in Israel! Thank God for the Philistine nobles who objected to it and kicked David out of the battle field. Otherwise, even now we would have conspiracy theorists claiming that it was David who killed Saul, not the Philistines.

Upon hearing this news, David mourned Saul and Jonathan publicly. He honored King Saul who spent much of his life chasing David, as much as possible. He wrote a song about them and taught them to the Israelites. He sent thank you note to the community that took the body of Saul and gave it a proper burial.

Many years later, when David came to know about the bones of Saul, David sent people to take them from there and bury them in Saul's homestead estate. (2 Samuel 21). We can see the caring heart of a child of God in all of these. (The validity of what he did that day is covered in detail in the chapter titled, 'The heart of a godly leader.') Now a door was divinely opened for David to move into the promises upon his life.

It is hard to believe that the seemingly unfortunate incident of Ziklag, where his own people were ready to stone David had anything to do with the transition stage that followed. Preachers always talk about how David revered it all. But David did more than that.

When David met the Amalekites, they were spread far and wide with sacks full of plunder under each tent. Certainly that did not come from David's camp! They were on pillage. A careful study of that chapter shows that they had gone all the way down to Egypt and plundered communities. They heard that the Philistines have gone to war with Israel and they plundered Philistine communities. So when David went and attacked them to recover their families and cattle, they came back with much more than they expected. Some people immediately became greedy and refused to share it with even other soldiers in their militia. Not David! As soon as he came into good times, he was ready to share it with others. We see him sending gifts to everyone who helped him in the past.

At that time, David did not even know that he was about to embark on the transition stage to becoming a king. But his act of generosity was well noted. For in 2 Samuel, chapter 2, when David sent the word that he is ready to come back and become the king, we see all of these people rising up to support him. This is a beautiful example of sowing and reaping. It is also proof for what the Bible teaches us in Romans 8:28. "And we know that all things work **together for good** to those who love God, to those who are the called according to His purpose." Even the mistakes in David's life worked together for good for him later! God is sovereign!!

Even after God did all of this to prepare the ground for David, he was not in a hurry. In 2 Samuel 2, we see him still asking the counsel of God. He started with a prayer meeting! "But seek first the kingdom of God and His righteousness, and all these things shall be added to you." (Mathew 6:33). He wanted to make sure that the steps he took were ordained by God.

He asked God, 'should I go to Judah?' God said go. Judah means praise. After the prayer time, he decided to go forward with praise. Judah was not where he was going to reign. He had already selected Jerusalem as his capital. Then, why did he go to Judah? David was a worshipper. He was always a worshipper. If he could worship God when he had nothing, in the midst of his sorrows, certainly there was praises in his life when he was about to ascend to the throne. He remembered that it was God who gave his this promise. It was God who sustained him in the darkest hours of his life. It was God who turned even his mistakes into blessings. He was not going to forget God now.

Then David went to Hebron and he was coroneted there. Originally it was a strong hold of the enemy, where the Anakims lived. It was such an imposing structure that the entire camp of Israel turned around and went back to the desert. But later it was captured under the leadership of Caleb. By the time of David, the place had a different meaning. Hebron meant fellowship then. So David is seeking Hebron.

David is looking for a group of people who want to shout with him and share in his joy. That is why you need to be part of a church. Many in the world go to a bar to celebrate their victory and pour out their heart to a bartender. People in the world are not crazy about your victories. The first thought in their mind is why did I not get it? They may try to sabotage you. Whereas, in the church, when you are among people who were upholding you when you were going through the dark days of your life, you will find a crowd who is genuinely happy about the turnaround in your life.

David still had a lot of issues to overcome since Saul left the scene in a vacuum. He left everything in a mess. He did not leave anyone in charge and people were all over in their thinking.

Three things stopped Saul from preparing his nation for change. First of all, he had a bloated ego. It came from the insecurity feeling he suffered from all his life. He could not think of a day when the nation could survive without him. The second problem was Saul's personal agenda. God had an agenda for the nation of Israel, which was revealed in the act of anointing David. But Saul wanted his son Jonathan to be the next king. To accomplish that he was ready to kill David. For thirty eight years Saul against the plan of God. So now, when Saul and Jonathan are dead, some people think it is someone from the household of Saul who should be the next king. Some others said God had rejected Saul a long time ago and anointed David, so David should be the next king. There was total confusion in the land and David had to handle it wisely. That is why he taking one step at a time and seeking God in all of these.

Thirdly, if Saul had seen value in God's choice, he would helped David (after all he was Saul's son in law) to groom into a future leader. Look at the testimonies about David in 1 Samuel 18. "So David went out wherever Saul sent him, and behaved wisely. And Saul set him over the men of war, and he was accepted in the sight of all the people and also in the sight of Saul's servants." (v.5). "And David behaved wisely in all his ways, and the LORD was with him." (v.14). "And so it was, whenever they went out, that David behaved more wisely than all the servants of Saul, so that his name became highly esteemed." (v.30). Everyone else can see value in David, except the leader who was supposed to groom him. We should not the word 'wisely' in all of these verses quoted above. The emerging leadership should use the opportunity that God gives them wisely. The existing leadership should recognize that trait in people. Also, David was the most faithful servant Saul had. But Saul never saw it that way.

Vacuum at the top will always create division. Alexander established the ancient Greek empire in a few years. But a few years later it was divided into four, since Alexander died without a child. The same was the story in Israel. Kingmakers began to emerge. Abner, who was the general of Saul's army, took one of the sons of Saul named Ishbosheth and made him king. Abner did not care what God wanted to do. (2 Samuel 2:8). Abner knew that David was already anointed king in Hebron. He did not care. He was ready to split the nation, hoping that only the tribe of Judah would follow David.

On side David is trying to make sure every step he took was in line with God. Or the other side, Abner was forcing his hand. So it was natural that there was unnecessary bloodshed in the land. (2 Samuel 2:19-32, 3:1). David was still not in a rush. He reigned in Hebron for over seven years waiting for God's time to become the ruler of the whole nation. Eventually God used the same man who split the nation, to unite the nation. It was under the leadership of Abner that the move started for the rest of the tribes to accept David. But Abner was killed and the process was delayed again. After some more bloodshed, none of which David had anything to do with; finally the nation was ready for David. (2 Samuel 5:1-3).

In that dark chapter, one can see that David was indeed a man after God's own heart. When Abner, the man who sowed the seed to split the nation, was killed by his own general Joab, David did not side with him. David in fact formally eulogized Abner. When Ishbosheth was killed in his by two of his servants and they brought his head to David, they expected a handshake and a royal gift. But David actually executed the men who killed Ishbosheth. He was always on the side of righteousness.

As soon as he became the king over the whole nation, David began to move in his vision. There is a verse in 1 Samuel 17 that we often overlook. "And David took the head of the Philistine and brought it to Jerusalem, but he put his armor in his tent." (v.54). It always surprised me. The war had nothing to do with Jerusalem. In fact, Jerusalem was inhabited by a people called Jebusites. So why did David take the head of Goliath to Jerusalem? He was declaring his vision!

The day he was anointed by Samuel, he knew he would become one day. He also knew that it would not happen in one day. But he started dreaming about and making plans about it. He selected Jerusalem to be his head quarters whenever he would become the king. Jerusalem was very strategically located on top of a hill 2000 feet high in the air.

On the first opportunity he got to tell the world about how he thought, he took the head of Goliath and walked past the armies of Israel all the way to Jerusalem sending the inhabitants a message. The same God who has helped me to have victory over this Philistine will give me victory over you. They did not get the message.

When David was making his move, the Jebusites who lived in Jerusalem looked down upon him and despised him. Because of their strategic advantages, they said, "You shall not come in here; but the blind and the lame will repel you," thinking, "David cannot come in here."Nevertheless David took the stronghold of Zion and turned it into the City of David.

What is your vision? You may be in a transition stage today. After much waiting, you can see that God is taking you to the next level. Where do you want to go? Do you have any plans? What are your dreams? What are you praying for?

Do not just sit in a throne like Saul. Develop visionary leadership like David and be ready to take the people of God to their destiny when God gives you the opportunity.

CHAPTER XI

Establishing the Throne—Part I

We have focused on the steps that David took as a godly leader chosen to lead a particular generation. We saw the wisdom in the things that he did. Now let us consider the challenges that come against leadership and how you can primarily handle that. The backdrop for our discussion will be 2 Sam. 5:17 onwards.

"Now when the Philistines heard that they had anointed (means Israel) David king over Israel, all the Philistines went up to search for David, and David heard of it and went down to the stronghold. The Philistines also went and deployed themselves in the Valley of Rephaim. So David inquired of the Lord saying, "Shall I go up against the Philistines? Will You deliver them into my hand?" And the Lord said to David, "Go up, for I will doubtless deliver the Philistines into your hand." So David went to Baal Perazim and David defeated them there. Before I continue I just want to tell you that the word breakthrough is found in the bible only in this place. "And he said the Lord has broken through my enemies before me, like a breakthrough of water." Therefore he called the name of that place Baal Perazim, which means where I got a breakthrough over Baal. And they left their images there, and David and his men carried them away. Then the Philistines went up once

again, and deployed themselves in the Valley of Rephaim. Therefore, David inquired of the Lord, He said, "You shall not go up; circle around behind them, and come up on them in front of the mulberry trees. And it shall be, when you hear the sound of the marching in the tops of the mulberry trees, then you shall advance quickly. For then the Lord will go out before you to strike the camp of the Philistines." And David did so, as the Lord commanded him and he drove back the Philistines from Geba as far as Gezer. "

When you are a leader, one of the first things you want to do is to bring unity. A leader cannot rule effectively if the people are not united. When king Saul was on the throne, he was dividing people. His efforts to create a division between David and Jonathan have already been discussed.

There are even some churches like that. Have you ever been to a church like that where the church is into so many different cliques? Everyone is in a different group and nobody can get together. Then they expect the church to flourish. No, that church will fall apart. If you look at the statistics in this country, there are hundreds of thousands of churches. The last account I had, someone made a list and said there were 380,000 churches. I am pretty sure it is more than that. But 85% of those churches have less than 85 people in the pews on a Sunday morning. At the same time we know that this is a land where we have churches with 20 to 30 thousand people. So what's the difference? If you go to any of these little churches, you may see that the pastor does everything. He may never allow someone else to do anything because he is so insecure like King Saul. Many times such leaders pit people against each other to maintain grip over the community. God is not in such a business.

Look at what David did to bring political unity and stability to his nation. First, he brought reconciliation between all tribes. In the first three verses, you see that after many years finally all the tribes got together. There was no longer this group verses that group. When everyone can get together you know that God is in it too.

The rebel leader Abner had established a division in the kingdom using a son of King Saul. But David did not go after him. He just waited for him to wake up and realize the mistake he made and waited for him to come to him. Sometimes you need to buy time, if you want to solve problems in your organization, home or business. If you want to make peace or reconcile things, the best thing to do is buy a little time. And David gave himself some time and waited because there is a time for peace

Secondly, we know that Abner was later killed by one of the people who were fiercely loyal to David. While this man Abner did not do anything good for David, even though Abner was the one who took the initiative to establish a counter throne in the kingdom, David eulogized him publicly and said I have nothing to do with his death. I am washing my hands. I will not side with injustice. When you are a leader it is extremely important to project the fact that you are a fair leader, that you do not show favoritism.

When Abner was killed, David could have been happy thinking that one headache is gone. That is not what David said. David eulogized him publicly and said he was a man of war. He was a hero. He was a talented man. This is not the way his life should have ended. When David did that there were ten tribes that were backing up Abner to establish that counter throne. At that time David had only two tribes with him. But just by handling that one situation wisely David won over the other ten tribes. The ten tribes sent word and said, 'Why are we divided like this? Why don't we get together? Why don't we establish David as king over all twelve tribes?'

Despite having leadership qualities, if you are not a fair leader and if you do not treat everyone the same, you will not have a big following. You will end up with a small group of people who are always bickering among themselves. But when the people see that you are a fair leader, and you handle things fairly and you give honor to the people who deserve honor, people will come to you. You will not have to go after people. Remember even when David was hiding in the cave, David did not go looking for people. They came to him because David was settled in the will of God.

The third thing that he did was reaching out to the house of King Saul. Remember the covenant part of his life and how he looked for anyone in the household of Saul to show compassion on behalf of the covenant that he entered into with Jonathan? Then they found out that there was a little boy, Jonathan's son who had survived the massacre that was taking place during that civil war. But when his nurse was running with him, the nurse fell into a ditch with him and he was paralyzed. His name was Mephiboshet and he was brought into the king's palace and was given a place next to the king on the royal table. That kind of mercy was unheard of in the old world. David had absolutely no reason to keep him alive. But he said because of the covenant that I have entered with your father you are going to eat at my table. Part of it is true about the covenant and part of it also wisdom on the part of David as the leader because he is reaching out to his enemy.

Since King Saul reigned in that nation as king and sat on the throne for forty years, irrespective of how anointed David was, how godly David was, how many victories he won for the nation of Israel, there was always a group of people who were always loyal to the family of Saul. Loyalty arises when you are a king because you have a payroll. Thousands of people are living off your payroll. All those people, despite the fact that King Saul was outside the will of Israel, always looked at him favorably because he fed them. When David came to the throne, if there was anyone left in that family, they should have been wiped out, which usually was what the kings did. They would wipe out everyone in that family and clean the slate and make sure that there would never ever be a person that would rise up from that lineage to challenge the new king or his children. If David acted selfishly like that, this kingdom would have always been divided. There would never be perfect unity in the kingdom. But David reached out to his enemy's family and said, "Is there someone left in this family that I may show mercy because of the covenant?"

How do you handle your situations? How do you make decisions? Some days you wonder how come I did not go further in life. How come we have not become a successful organization? How come I am not successful in business? You have to learn to treat people well. The best leaders in the world are the leaders who know how to treat people. Why do you think all the people want to work for Google?

Somebody gave me a Maxwell Leadership Bible as a gift, written by John Maxwell, the best known leadership guru in Christianity. He has written so many books on leadership. When we come to 2 Samuel, chapter 5, Maxwell gives us five important points about vision. I thought I will bring them to your attention to illuminate what we have been discussing.[1]

1. **<u>Vision unites people</u>**.
   When all twelve tribes came behind David, they were not only united behind a man but they were united behind a vision. That is why vision is so important. That is why the word of God says, 'where there is no vision people perish' (Proverbs 29:18 KJV). You need to know what you are following. All the problems do not have to be solved for people to follow you. You do not have to have a perfect answer to every question for people to follow you. But people need direction in their life. They need to know where they are going.

   When we established Gateway with the help of God, the first thing we did was to come up with a vision statement. We clearly stated our vision. But our vision is simply put, to raise up a new generation of believers in this post modern part of the United States called Long Island where majority of the people do not go to church. We have taken it as a challenge to raise up a generation that will go to church, that will read the Bible, that will study the Bible, that will stand up

---

[1] John C. Maxwell, The Maxwell Leadership Bible, Second edition(Knoxville, Thomas Nelson Publishers, 2007), 378.

for the faith to which they are committed at any cost. That is the vision of our church. So when people started coming here, one of the first things they asked me was, "Pastor, where is this church going?" I had to have an answer. I could not say, "I don't know yet, I am still praying about it." People would immediately say if the leader does not know where he is taking the people why should the people follow him? So it is vision that unites people.

2. Vision provides a center for leadership.

What was that center for David? It was Jerusalem! He called all the people who used to look at that stronghold and wishfully think that David could occupy that. David committed to conquer it. He knew it was a huge challenge, but committed to it and rallied the people around it. Jerusalem was going to be their political and spiritual center during the reign of David. It was this vision of David that provided a center for leadership.

3. Vision dominates our conversation.

Do you guys talk to yourself? I do. Sometimes my wife asks me, 'What did you say?' I say, 'nothing' because it is not for her but for me. What did you tell yourself last week? Did you tell yourself, 'Oh my life . . . ? I want to beat myself up . . . . It is not going anywhere . . . . It is going downhill . . . . I can feel the arteries coming up . . . . There is pain in all the joints in my body . . . . I haven't slept well for two months . . . . I don't know how long this is going to last.' Don't! You are digging a premature grave for yourself.

You need to learn to talk to yourself the right way. You have to be sure of where you are going before you tell somebody else to come along with you. If you do not know where you are going why should I join you in the journey? Why do you think thousands of people followed Jesus Christ? He always knew where He was going. The Bible says he was always sure of what he was going to do next. Start talking positively to yourself. More than half of the Psalms are the psalmists exhorting themselves. And sometimes they will say negative things about themselves like 'the enemy is encamped against me, they are lying in wait for my soul' etc. But then they will realize that at the same time they are children of God. And they will change the language and say, 'I shall fear no evil, for thou art with me.' I am not alone in this. God is with me, I do not have to worry. Things do not look good in the natural but I do not worry. I am not going to end like this.

Turn your attention to a man who lived thousands of years ago named Job in the Bible. He lost everything that he had. He was a wealthy man but he became a pauper. He had ten sons but all ten sons were killed. Then he began to lose his health. He was covered with boils and the flies were flocking his body. He had to sit in ashes to prevent the flies from landing on his body. Can you imagine someone with boils sitting in ashes? And from morning until night all he did was scratch himself. Nobody could stand him. Even his wife gave up on him and said let us commit suicide. Initially, he also had some negative thoughts that you can read about in the book of Job. Later on, as he continued to talk to himself, he realized, 'Yes, everything is against me. I lost everything I used to have at one time. I lost all the money; I lost all the cattle I had in the fields. I lost the children. I lost my health. But still I am a child of God!! He can give me everything back.'

That is where your recovery begins! You have to tell yourself even though everything else is stacked up against you; you are still a child of God! Job became emboldened in faith and he started to claim, 'one day I will see my redeemer with my own eyes.'

When faith comes back to you everything else will follow. That is why the enemy wants to rob your faith. That is why he comes after you with issues after issues, so your faith will be stolen and you will have no time but to complain. Even then have boldness to say 'I may be going through all of this, but I am a child of God.' In order to do that though, you need to know where you are going. You have to have vision in life. You have to believe what God has told you.

All of you are promise carriers. God has told you where he wants to take you. Do you believe that? Or have you given up on that vision? Once you give up on that vision, there is no way you can change the language of your inner conversation. But if you believe, if you hold on to what God has promised you, vision will help you to change your inner conversation.

4. **Vision will always inspire greatness.**
   Greatness comes from vision. Greatness does not come from education, or from money or from your lineage but from vision. All you need is vision and the confidence that inspires within you.

Years ago, one young congressman in this country stood for election and lost the election. Everyone looked at him and said, 'You are not political material, don't waste your time.' But this young man, who happened to be a Christian, had a vision. He knew in order for him to carry out what God was inspiring him to do, he had to reach a certain level. And he knew in his mind what he wanted to do when he got there. He kept fighting against all the odds. He did not have money but knew where he wanted to get to. He had decided in his mind that slavery is against the Bible and against Christian principles. He would stop slavery in this country. But he knew there was no way he could do that as a small time lawyer in Chicago. He had to become the president of this nation before he could change the laws. So he fought and allowed that vision to carry him until one day he became president and declared the emancipation of the slaves. Today, when we look back at history, every single person acknowledges Abraham Lincoln as one of the greatest presidents this nation ever had. His power source was vision.

A young lawyer from India went to South Africa to make money and to represent the Indian community there. He saw the injustice done to the people in South Africa in the form of apartheid, and he gave up his very lucrative job as a young lawyer. He started a movement there to stand up against the injustices.

He came back to the nation of India to end the political subjugation of that land. He had gone to South Africa with a three piece suit. He came back with a three piece suit and when he landed in India he realized, 'I am an Indian but I do not know India.' He decided to travel throughout India in train. He wanted to identify with the people. So he gave up his suit. He travelled in third class compartments of the train. People only had very scanty clothes. So he gave up the suit and traveled with just one piece of cloth, called the dhoti, and just wrapped it around him. He even gave up the shirt and never wore even an undershirt after that. He traveled all over the nation to learn about the people. He inspired a generation to stand up against the mighty empire of Great Britain. His moral courage influenced so many including Martin Luther King and Nelson Mandela. What empowered him? Vision!

He would walk around with that one piece of cloth just wrapped around him. Thousands of people were killed during the struggle for independence from Great Britain. In 1947 without taking a sword in their hand, without committing terrorism, just by the power of their vision they overcame the mighty Great Britain. Today when we look at this man, the entire world calls him Mahatma. Mahatma means great soul. What made him great? Vision made him great.

There is greatness in you just as there was greatness in David. When David started as a shepherd boy even in his family he was ostracized. Nobody saw greatness in him except God. When God gave him opportunities he used it wisely. We can see him building himself up until he became the greatest king that the nation of Israel ever had in history.

Do you know there is greatness in you? In every boy and every girl, there is greatness. You may be in your fifties or sixties and may say, 'My life is over. I wish somebody shared this message with me twenty years ago so I would have done something.' No, you do not need a lot of time. Do you know how many years apostle Paul ministered before he died? Fifteen years! In fifteen years he changed the history of the world. He wrote two-thirds of the New Testament. Do you know there is greatness in you? But you have to hold on to your vision to reach greatness. What is your vision?

Finally, vision is what attracts people to a leader. When people see a leader with vision, people will come. All the ten tribes who were against David changed their mind because they could see that this man was a visionary leader. They knew he would take them forward. When you have vision, others will come and join you and strengthen your hands, making it easier to reach where God is taking you. True, you have to get to a certain level, before you can fully carry out what God has inspired you to do. But know that God will strengthen you to fulfill your call.

CHAPTER XII

Establishing the Throne—Part 2

We will go back to 2 Samuel 5 and 6 once again to learn some more lessons from there.

We are discussing the steps David took to establish his leadership position. For you it may be a position in your office, your position as a supervisor or the manager or the next level that you are going up to. How can we handle the opportunities that God gives us wisely, to establish ourselves in the position that God wants us to reach? That is what this study is all about and we are using David as a backdrop to learn these lessons.

This lesson is equally applicable to everyone whether you are a child of God or not because it is all about vision. We know that vision is necessary for General Motors as much as a child of God. We know all the mess they found themselves in, in recent years was because of the lack of vision. I remember in the 80's we had long gas lines and everyone was starting to make small cars. I remember standing in those gas lines with my little Chevette. The gas was rationed and when you got all the way to the front they said you could only buy $5 worth of gas that day because they had to give to everyone. I remember those days. But then all of a sudden, things changed and there was a glut of gasoline in the market.

American car companies had stated making small cars. But as soon as the gas price went down, the vision changed. All of a sudden people started feeling that it was going to remain this way forever. Instead of starting to refine the smaller cars they started and making them better, they started producing gas guzzlers and started only focusing on US market. This is where there was easy money. They did not have to ship the cars anywhere, just put it on a truck and bring it to a dealer. So what happened? The vision changed. I should actually say the vision faded or I should say there was no vision. Somehow, people got the notion that the good times were going to last forever and there would always be a glut of gasoline in the market. We saw the SUVs getting bigger and bigger. All of a sudden you saw one person driving an SUV as big as a bus in third world countries, for one person to go to work. And that was a total waste of gasoline and resources.

Nobody was thinking long term and when the economy changed they were so ill prepared for what was out there. They had absolutely no back-up plan. One day, we found the Chairman of GM standing in front congress begging for a loan from the government to avoid bankruptcy. Even then they could not. Vision is equally important in the secular world.

I like reading books written by leaders, and I was reading this book written by Jack Welsh, detailing his memoirs about leaving GE. We can see how he made that company into a global powerhouse and it was all based on vision.

Vision is necessary for everyone. Even if you are a student, you need vision. You still need to have an idea of where you are going with your life. Only then can you focus and channel your energy to accomplish the goals that you have set for yourself. Every business needs vision. Every church needs vision. Vision is equally applicable to Christians and non-Christians. But there are some other things that the world does not pay any attention to that as Christians we need to focus on.

If you are a child of God you have to understand certain spiritual principles. In 2 Samuel 5, we saw that David waited for a long time to become the king. He received the anointing as a young man and he had a vision at that time, about what he was going to do. He knew it would not be the next day but if the anointing was on him, he will definitely become the king one day. He was always guided by that vision.

We saw a manifestation of that vision when he killed Goliath and he took the head of Goliath and traveled all the way to Jerusalem and plastered it on the city walls of Jerusalem even though Jerusalem had nothing to do with Israel at that time. It was occupied by another tribe at that time. In other words, he was actually declaring his vision. David was saying, 'This is my vision. When I become the king, Jerusalem is going to become my capital. I am declaring that in front of all you today. Today it may be occupied by another tribe called Jebusites but I am coming here. I will take this place. I will make this my headquarters.' That is the power of vision!

We saw at the beginning of 2 Samuel 5, that he accomplished that vision with the help of people. The Bible says that David himself knew that God has established him because he got his throne, he got his city and a neighboring king was sending laborers free of charge at the other kings expense to build a palace for him. That is when you know God's favor is upon you when some other king say you are a new king and you need a palace. You have just conquered the city but you have nothing there. I am going to send my laborers at my expense to build a palace for you. That is what is called favor! How many of you know that it is better to have God's favor than to have good health? It is better to have God's favor than to have a lot of money in the bank. Favor makes everything possible. If God's favor is upon your life, everything becomes possible.

One day when I was watching Daystar when they were having a share-a-thon. On one of the episodes and they were telling us how God put a little dream in their heart to reach the city of Alabama. They got a little cable channel there and that is how Daystar was born. They were running it from their apartment, empowered by the vision. Then, God gave them favor and people started showing up and investing money in the vision. Before they knew it, Daystar was all over the world. If you go to the Middle East, Christian television is all over the Middle East beaming programs into these Muslims homes. If they have a satellite dish they can watch many Christian programs as many times as they need. You know when you look at the history of all these ministries you can see that it was not their money, it was not because they were multi millionaires. It was always the favor of the Lord that made it possible.

So if the favor of the Lord is upon your life, you are going to go places! Boldly, make a proclamation about your life. "I'm going to go somewhere because the favor of the Lord is upon me". Let it be a faith proclamation about your life.

One day David was a little boy chasing sheep and then he was a king of a nation. What made it possible? Not his wisdom, not his ability but his faith and the favor of the Lord. But at the same time you have to realize this: If you are a child of God you have an enemy who cannot stand to see you succeed in life. Here is David, after decades of waiting, finally getting established and here comes the enemy. Look back at the passage 2 Samuel 5. "When the Philistines heard that they had or Israel had anointed David king over Israel, all the Philistines went up to search for David."

Isn't that interesting? When David was struggling the Philistines were willing to join with David. When David was running around, the Philistines actually used him as a mercenary, as a militia for hire. They had nothing against David until David got his throne. When they heard that David became king they decided it was time to stop him. We never thought he would go this high.

Nobody cares if you go a little further in your life. Nobody cares if you reach a financial status where you do not have to pay your monthly bills using your credit card. Nobody cares when you get one little promotion. But watch out when God raises you up to greater heights. It is at this time that an enemy who cannot stand that will come against you. The question that we want to address today is how will you handle that enemy coming against you.

A lot of thoughts went through my mind when I was going through this. First of all, where did David start his public life, confronting Philistines! The first victory in his life was defeating a Philistine giant called Goliath. Now along the way we saw he had struggles many times against the Philistines. But today here come Philistines again.

This is something that confuses the children of God. We believe in spiritual warfare, we know that it is a reality. We know that the enemy is out there. But sometimes we wonder, how many times we need to take victory in our lives before the enemy will actually leave us alone. Have you ever been there? You take victory in one area and you think 'yes, finally I got victory, I can relax' only to see the enemy coming again. The same enemy keep coming again and again and you ask 'Lord, how many times should I take victory before I can finally be sure that I have victory. Well, unfortunately, I only have one answer for you—none of us have reached that point yet!

So you better wake up because the enemy will come at you again because the enemy sees God lifting you up to greater heights. If the enemy plans to target you again, don't get discouraged. Just realize that even before you understand where God is taking you, the enemy sometimes understands where you are going. So if the enemy is targeting you today it's only because you are important. He can see that your influences are increasing. He can see that you keep expanding your horizons. He can see that, if I leave this person is left alone like this it is going to be too difficult for me to pull him down later so let me do this right now.

If you are a child of God, this is the reality of life. One battle is not enough sometimes. That is why the Bible says we are in a battlefield. We must be equipped and we must adorn the spiritual weapons that are available for us. We must always be ready to fight the good fight because you do not know when the enemy is going to unleash war against you. You have to be vigilant.

When the enemy came against David, they filled a valley called Rephaim. The meaning of the word Rephaim is giant. David started his life, by killing one giant. But one day when he woke up and looked over the hill into the valley over Jerusalem, and he saw a valley full of giants. Remember when one giant would shout, everyone would look for a cave to hide in, starting from the king in Israel. If one giant could initiate so much terror, imagine a valley full of giants. What do you do when you see a valley full of giants standing up against your life?

The giant in your life may not be a physical person. That valley may be a pile of bills. Your valley may be filled with unpaid bills. Your valley may be filled with health issues. What do you do then as a child of God? Well, what did David do? David went back to God and asked for guidance. That is also your answer! If you keep your eyes upon the giants all day long, you will only get frustrated. People will murmur in your ears, "You see all those giants? If we could not stand one giant how are we going to come against a valley full of giants?" And they will kill your confidence. They will kill your faith. They will kill your worship. Everything will be gone.

Whatever is the giant pressing against you, do not focus on that all day long because that it not your place as a child of God. I am not asking you to pretend that it is not there. You acknowledge that it is there. Then you go to the presence of God and say 'Lord, I know it is there. You are the one who brought me this far and you are the one who is going to take me from here. Tell me how to handle all these giants that are lining up against me. I need Your advice. I need a word from you. I need to hear from you today.' He will speak into your life. How much of a desire do you have to hear a word from the Lord today?

God gave guidance to David. As soon as God spoke into his life, David became very strong against the entire valley full of giants. He defeated them in no time. Look at verse 20, this is what David said, "the Lord has broken through my enemies before me like a breakthrough of water." Do you know what that means? When David got that word from God that He would give him victory, David expected a long and protracted battle. It doesn't matter how many giants are lined up against you, if God is promising your victory, your victory will come in no time. David was ready to go for a protracted battle but he did not have to and he was surprised.

You may be very discouraged in your life. Maybe you had many battles in your life already and you are probably already discouraged seeing more enemies lined up against you. You probably think that you are never going to have victory. When God shows up, victory does not take a long time. Until God shows up, it is going to be prolonged and you have to spend a lot of time, going through the motions but when God shows up your victory comes so quickly that you will be surprised.

God gave David the victory so fast that the enemy camp did not have enough time to take everything that they brought with them back to their land because they were all running for their lives. So David went after them to plunder their camp. When he went into their camp he saw graven images everywhere. Spiritual battle does not happen in a vacuum. Spiritual battle needs a power source. David used to wonder, 'what is wrong with the Philistines? Why do they keep coming after me again and again? I am minding my own business. I am not fighting against them. I am just trying to establish my throne here. Why do they keep coming up after me again and again?' Let me tell you why, because there was somebody propelling them. There was a power source and it was the gentile worship system.

Spiritual Warfare does not happen in a vacuum, there is a power source behind it. And unless you identify the power source and take victory over that power source, you cannot have victory. In one of my trips to South Africa, I was praying in a little church service and it had about thirty-five people that night, it was a small church. At the end of the service somebody brought a man who was in his fifties at that time. He was a very heavy set man. One look and I could see that he had some mental issues. So they brought him to the front for prayer. He used to do very well for himself. He was a very successful businessman. Nobody knows what happened to him.

When I was about to pray for him, I noticed that there was a string on his hand. It is a Hindu thing, they attach mantras to that. I saw that string and God told me that is the reason he is sick because it has brought demonic presence into his life. I told them that I will pray but they have to let me cut that string. Initially they were reluctant and then they said yes. We cut it and burned it in front of them right there and then we prayed and I left. The next night I see a much bigger crowd about two hundred people in that little church. I was wondering what happened? I knew that God did something.

At the end of my message I gave an altar call and I saw a whole bunch of people coming forward. When I went to pray for them every one of them stretched out their hand. They all had that string on their hand. Many of them were from the family of the man I prayed for the previous night. That had received his deliverance. And they knew that the Pastor had cut the string and negated the power source that was making him sick. Instead of bowing down like we do, they all stretched forth their hands and said do the same for us. I cut a lot of strings that day. We had a nice little bon fire there burning all those things up. All of them became believers and are still members in that church worshipping God and walking in victory.

There are power sources behind spiritual warfare. Identify the power source behind your spiritual battle because something is fueling it. Something is sending this power against you again and again and again. Until you identify that power source and take victory over that power source, your battle cannot be over.

David was surprised, a valley full of graven images. As a child of God he knew, no wonder these people were coming up against me again and again. He gathered them to another side and I'm pretty sure he burned it all up to ashes and probably thought the battle was over.

But then when we read that passage we can see that they came up against him again. Because they want revenge for their gods. You think you got victory trusting in your God? We will show you the power of our Gods. Anytime that Mr. Carmel is prepared you don't have to worry because victory is guaranteed for you. There is only one true living God in this universe! All of these people came against David and said, you took all of our gods and reduced them to ashes. We will show you! We will take revenge for our Gods! And God said ok, now the battle is not between you and the Philistines. The battle has become between Me and their gods. So God said, David, this time you don't have to do the battle because the battle has changed. God said, David, just do this, go behind them and watch for my lead by the mulberry trees. When you hear my armies marching over the mulberry trees you just walk behind them into your victory!

David obeyed the counsel of God and had a resounding victory. It also became a turning point in his life. "Then the fame of David went out into all lands, and the LORD brought the fear of him upon all nations." (1 Chro. 14:17) Only after you have defeated the enemy completely can your growth take off.

CHAPTER XIII

A New Encounter with God

Even though his throne was established, the palace was established, David being a worshipper became unhappy. How do we know that? Read Psalm 132:3-5. This is another proof that God does not make mistakes. Because if you are a person who have been going around in circles for many years having no idea where your life is going and finally you get established and you get your throne and somebody comes and builds a palace at their expense for your sake, you will be enjoying it for a while before you start thinking about anything else. I will have a million different excuses. I will say I paid my dues. Do you know how many years it is since I laid my head on a pillow? I have been sleeping somewhere on a stone for so many years. Thank God for king Hiram, I am going to enjoy this palace for a while, and then we will worry about everything else. But that was not David.

This is what David said in Psalm 132:3-5, "Surely I will not go into the chamber of my house, or go up to the comfort of my bed, I will not give sleep to my eyes or slumber to my eyelids until I find a place for the Lord, a dwelling place for the mighty one of Jacob." Is it any wonder that God corrected Samuel when he went into the household of Jesse and said, "Samuel, you look at the outside, you look at the height of the people, you look at the weight of the people, you look at the stature of the people but I look at the heart of people. And I know how to measure the heart of a person." A young king in his prime youth is saying, "I will not get into my bed". He said, "I will not put slumber to my eyelids".

He said I will not even close my eyes until God shows me a way to bring glory to this God who has elevated me from the pastures. I know I had a tough road coming up here. I know it was not easy coming up here but I am here anyway! He has brought me this far anyway! At least some of us can identify with David. We were not born into this world with silver spoons in our mouth. Our life has been tough. The road that we came through has been tough. We have overcome so much but nonetheless he has proved himself to be a faithful God.

David had been waiting for this blessed day. He knew this day would come. 'I always believed this day would come but now that the day is here, I want to give God the glory before I start enjoying my blessings.' He decided to put God first. That is what Jesus taught us to do. Seek ye first the kingdom of God and his righteousness and all other things will be added to you.

David wanted to bring glory to God. How do I do that? The first thought that came to his mind was 'while I am enjoying this palace, God's ark, and the symbol of God's presence with the nation of Israel is sitting in the house of a man called Abinadab.'

Let me give you a little bit of background. The ark was taken by gentiles in the battle we read about in 1 Samuel, chapter 4. The Philistines took it and put it their temple thinking that there were magical powers to the ark. It became a curse for them so they sent it back on a cart pulled by two milking cows. And when the ark came to the borders of Israel, the cows stopped. So the Israelites went to get it and they had no idea what to do with the ark. So they took the cows and offered the cows as a sacrifice to God. And took the ark and put it in somebody's house in that border town. Instead of God being the center of their life, God is at the border.

Is not that what is happening with our lives many times? Instead of God being at the center of your life, (I would not say God is not in your life), but He is somewhere at the border. God is the last thing in your list of priorities. If I have time left after my job, after my beauty shop, after my nail salon, after everything else, I may show up on Sunday morning. But do not expect me to come any other days. Even Sunday morning is not easy for me. If I have time after everything else, I will show up. Isn't that where some of us are? I invite you to take a stock of your life.

We are no better than the Israelites, keeping God at the border. In case we get in trouble, we want to know where He is so we can run to Him. But when everything else is going good, we don't care. Let the ark stay in Abinadab's home. And it stayed there for at least twenty years. Based on the way you calculate the years some people say it stayed there for seventy years because it was caught at the beginning of the ministry of Samuel. Samuel ministered for almost forty years and then Saul reigned for almost forty years. In the book of Acts, when that story is reiterated it says twenty years. So let us go with twenty years, the lower number. So at least for twenty years, nobody cared about God.

Since the time Saul assumed the throne there were issues after issues in the country. But Saul never once went to the Ark. It was a leadership that did not care about God. They wanted all the problems solved. This is a message for our nation also. We want all of our problems solved. People are discussing issues on different TV channels, but what is the answer? The answer is the Ark!

But we as a nation do not want the Arc to come to the center. The answer is God and God is ready to help us out but we do not want God in the center. We have established clauses in the form of separation of church and state to make sure that God will not be allowed at the center of our dealings. God should not be in our schools. God should not be in our courtrooms. God should not be in Congress. At the same time we keep God at an arm's length. We may not pass a law saying that the churches cannot exist. We may not pass a law saying that Sunday morning people should not go to church.

But at the same time we do not want God at the center of our lives. We just want to be able to find him on days like September eleven, 2001.

David said no, not during my watch! This is the importance of godly leadership. As soon as the godly leader came on the throne, he said, 'I am going to bring the glory back. I am going to bring the Ark back. And even before I start enjoying my palace, I want to make sure that I bring God back and establish His presence properly. Only after that will I enjoy the blessings that God has given me.'

When we read 2 Samuel, chapter 6, we can see the first attempt of David to bring the ark back. It failed. Why? David chose thirty thousand people to bring the Ark back. He knew the Ark was out there and he needed to bring it to Jerusalem, to establish it at the center of their national life. Personally, he was a worshipper. He wanted to be able to run into the presence of God and worship Him. Sometimes you can have good intentions, sometimes you can be a man of God, a woman of God and still make mistakes.

The first attempt of David fizzled out. Not because God did not want to come back into the life of the nation of Israel. Not because God did not want His ark to come to Jerusalem. Not because God had anything against David. Even though David's intentions were good, the methods were wrong. So when you serve God and when you want to follow God it is important to have good intentions, but also to follow the methods that He has established for us.

Thirty thousand people and David were going as a big procession to the border town and a few feet into the nation of Philistines. What is David doing here? It is a show of people power.

David is coming to that border land with the thirty thousand people basically sending a message to the Philistines saying this is not the same old tiny Israel anymore. I am the king here, God has established me. I am bringing God back into my presence but at the same time I want you to know that we are a powerful nation now. So it is an exhibition of people power. If you read the passage you can see that there are so many names mentioned about the princes among the people, the wealthiest among the people. The key supporters of David, all of them are mentioned there but one group of people is really missing—the Levites. The people who were supposed to carry the Ark are missing! So in the first attempt the Levites were marginalized.

David thought, 'I know how to worship God. I am a worshipper. I am going to go in my power and I am going to carry musical instruments and establish a choir and make a lot of noise. We are going to shout through the streets and we are going to bring this Ark back on our terms. And it is going to be a show of our power.' Where are the Levites? Not mentioned at all! Maybe a few of them were among them. But they had no role to play in that entire episode.

God kept quiet. Even without God you can put up a nice show for God. Sometimes when I watch some of the church services, I know they are putting up a nice show for God even though nobody cares where God is in it or not. God will not come and interrupt your service even if you are not doing it properly or scripturally. He will stay in the background and He will keep quiet. But I want you to understand something. There comes a moment where the truth will come out.

In the account in 2 Samuel, we do not read about the oxen. But, the same story is given to us in 1 Chronicles 15 in a little more detail. The cart was actually drawn by oxen. David is looking into history and saying this is the way the Philistines sent the Ark over here. They had a cart and they had two cows, instead of cows I am going to put oxen there. And then two names are mentioned there, one of them being Uzzah. Uzzah was the son of Abinadab.

So there are two boys from the house where the Ark was for twenty years. And these two boys are sitting on that bullock cart and they are the drivers. You know if two oxen are pulling a cart, is it a bullock cart. David is shouting at the top of his lungs in front of that Ark and the choir is there with a lot of musical instruments. It was indeed a noisy affair. And it went on until it came to Nakhon's threshing floor.

We have seen another threshing floor that it was within the borders of the city of Jerusalem. And we learned that even though it is called a threshing floor, it is not really a threshing floor. Because when they made worship places for fertility gods at that time they made it like a threshing floor. People would bring grain there and give it as an offering to their fertility god or goddess. Why did the oxen stumble at that particular point? The oxen were going good, going straight until it came to this place called Nakhon's threshing floor. I believe that that was a worship place for a pagan deity; a worship place for their fertility god. So the satanic presence was there. The opposition was there. Everything went smooth until they came face to face with a spiritual opposition.

You can put up a nice show for God. You can serve God with your talents. You can serve God with your abilities. You can say, 'I have preaching ability. I was always a speaker so I can speak.' But if God is not within me I am just putting up a show for Him. And people will be impressed. It was an impressive sight in Israel that day. Thirty-thousand people dancing in the street will be always an impressive sight. The king was a musician taking the harp in his hand and playing on the harp and it was an impressive sight. But let me tell you, if you are interested in only putting up a show, it will only last until you hit the first bump of spiritual opposition against you, against your life, against your ministry. As soon as the spiritual opposition comes the show comes to a screeching halt.

Satan always infiltrates in unexpected ways. The Arc was Abinadab's home and Uzzah and his brother were custodians of the Ark for at least twenty years. They were a family with the Ark. They were properly taking care of the Ark. Familiarity always gets us in trouble because as soon as the oxen stumbled Uzzah looked back and became concerned for God. And he reached out and tried to stabilize the Ark and immediately God killed him. Why? All the man did was stabilizing the Ark.

There are a number of spiritual lessons we have to learn from this passage. First of all, the opposition can stumble us, but it cannot stumble God. One month things do not go the way we expect and we start getting nervous and even though we are children of God we start wondering, where is God?

I preached a message once from the book of Revelation. In the midst of all those things that were creating chaos all over the world, all God did was tell John to come up here. God did not give him an explanation. God elevated John in the spirit all the way into His throne room up in heaven, the first thing that he was shown was the throne of God and God still sitting on the throne. God was sending a message to John. He was saying, 'John, waves after waves of judgment are going to come on the face of the earth. Things are going to change, things are going to stumble, nations will fall, islands will disappear, and nuclear bombs will fall all over the world and 2/3 of the earth will be burning up in fire. But in the midst of all of that, John, never forget that I am still on my throne. Nothing will move me.' That's why David wrote, 'your throne is established forever. '

When the spiritual opposition comes and tries to stumble you, instead of you trying to stabilize it, all you have to do as a worshipper is just look to God. Nothing would have happened to that Ark that day. It is God's Ark and God knows how to take care of His Ark. You and I are custodians of God's presence. The Bible tells us, "know you not, you are the temple of God and the spirit of God lives in you?" But it does not mean that I have to do something carnally to keep it there. It is entirely up to God. That is why God killed Uzzah. Not because God had anything against this young man. So we have to learn to serve God fearfully. Some of us need a new encounter with God.

We have to go back to God because He has become too familiar to us. We have lost the fear of God. We have lost the respect for God. We have lost the awe of God. We walk around as if God is in our pocket. We lost the fear of God. Look at our generation. I am not a judgmental person, I am not a legalistic person, but when I see ministers taking God for granted it really makes me concerned. I wish we can come back to the fear of God. If we do not, God will do something to bring in the fear of God. And then we will all complain against God. God, why did you do that? And that is exactly what happened to David. At the end of that story it tells us that that day David feared God. Why, David was a worshipper, a true worshipper. Taking things for granted, taking the things of God lightly, we cannot do that. We do not have the privilege to do that!

The second problem of the story was putting the Ark on a new cart. When I was developing this, that word, the "new cart" began to stick out in my mind because that has been the perennial mistake in the church. We are no longer satisfied by old fashioned gospel. We do not want to hear the old style messages anymore. We do not want to sing the old hymns. We do not want to identify with the fathers and the grandfathers who kept the church alive for two thousand years. Today the church is more interested in a "new cart". Everyone is looking for a "new cart". In today's world if a church wants to stand out, it is not sticking to the Word of God that makes the church stand out. It's creating a "new cart". So the churches have become so varied in our generation. Some people say, I go to that church because that church has wonderful worship. Now when they say wonderful worship it may not mean that the spirit of God is moving in that worship. It means that it is a wonderful show, a music show with stage lighting extravaganza.

It cost about $50,000 for one set of background for the stage these days. And if you follow Christian television regularly and look at the background they use, almost every six months they are changing the backgrounds. You know why? In order to keep the people in the church there must be a "new cart". There must be something new all the time. Otherwise people say same old same old. I don't want to go to that church anymore. It has been a mistake in the church all along. And when we put the emphasis on building new carts, all kinds of churches pop up. If you make a study of where Christianity is today, you will be amazed at how many weird doctrines are out there. Many churches do not care about the doctrinal purity anymore. Very few churches really preach the true word. People do not want the word. And when we say this people will say you are too hard. No, we are just being faithful to the word of God. So we refuse to create "new carts".

Today we know that people are no longer satisfied with the four gospels that are found in the bible. Everyone is digging up new gospels. They are looking through Dead Sea scrolls and other sources for this. After you read the four gospels, you want to know more about God and you do some research I have nothing against it. But these days people do not want to follow the gospel message. Because the gospel says, 'unless you are born again you will not enter into the kingdom of God.' But nobody wants to hear that.

Jesus asked us teach the people and baptize those who believe. Teach the people about the Holy Spirit. Nobody wants to take baptism. But everyone is interested in the gospel of Thomas or gospel of Mary and they are always trying to dig up new stuff and create controversies. Then they say this Bible says this and your Bible says that, so I do not have to follow either one. Trying to escape what God is asking us to do. Creating "new carts."

We compromise . . . until God reaches out one day and puts his divine scare in us.

God is not against new things. So when God say establish things as the Bible says, He is talking about things that you have no right to change. For example, I have no right to change the doctrine of salvation. The doctrine of baptism, I have no right to change. The doctrine of infilling of the Holy Spirit, I have no right to change. The doctrine of the return of Jesus Christ, I have no right to change. The doctrine of Jesus coming back as King of this world, I have no right to change. But people are changing it and creating new carts all the time. Everyone is looking for something new?

That also is not a new phenomenon. In Acts 17, the Bible tells us that when Apostle Paul went into the city of Athens for the very first time there was this Mars hill where all the philosophers would get together and discuss various things. And concerning the crowd that he met there, even though they were learned, the Bible tells us that they were only interested to see if there is something new. So when Paul started talking, they said, oh, this is something new. He is talking about Jesus. Where is this Jesus from? But at the end of that message though, they only wanted novelty. They did not want to know Jesus. So at the end of that conversation they all started making fun of Apostle Paul. And he walked away completely discouraged.

And when he came to the city of Corinth, God had to send his angel to come and strengthen him and tell him, 'fear not, just preach the word.' If you go after novelty, if you go after churches that are after novelty let me tell you they only want novelty. They are not after God.

What is more important to you? God or novelty? So the Bible tells us very clearly again, that God has shown you which way to go. And all we have to do is go that way. But a good thing about a worshipper is that he/she always learns from their mistakes.

David knew he made a mistake and he decided to learn from his mistake. 2 Samuel 6, verses 6 and 9, it tells us that David was afraid of the Lord that day. And he started doing something that he should have done the first time. Even though the first time his intention was good, he failed to do something that he used to do all the time. Before he would do anything, he would go to God and ask His guidance. But the first time he tried to bring the ark back, he said, I am bringing God's presence back. Then why do I need to ask God? So he went out and did things in a wrong way, ended up in judgment and let the ark stay in another man's home. But when he came to his senses he decided to learn from his mistake. He started asking God. In the last part of verse 9, he says, how should I bring the ark to the city? He started asking questions.

We have also made mistakes in our lives. Sometimes we make mistakes in the way we handle things of God. And when you make a mistake all you have to do is sit in the presence of God and earnestly seek his counsel and He will give you His counsel. And then you will understand the mistake you have made. David realized the mistakes that he made. There are three things that are given to us in the Bible. David said, in the King James Bible it says, "We sought him not after the due order". In the New King James Bible, it says, "We did not consult Him about the proper order".

When you do God's business, understand that it is God's business and make sure you consult with Him. 'How should I do it?' And follow the instructions that He gives you. And I like the way New Living Translation puts it, 'we failed to ask God how to move the ark in a proper way.' David understood that he made a mistake. So he decided to do things in a new order. And these are the things that he did, as we see in 1 Chronicles 15.

First thing he did was sanctification. This is the beauty of spending time in the presence of God. Every time you go back to God you realize that I have no right to do anything, unless God uses me for a specific purpose. And He prepares us for it. We know there are people out there in the world that take the Bible and throw the Bible around. They can do all of that because they are not bound by it. They are outside the covenant. But as a child of God, bought by the precious blood of the Lamb of God, I cannot take that kind of liberty with this Bible. Every morning, when I get up and pray in the morning, I pray, 'Lord, make me worthy to take this Bible in my hands today.' When I get to church on Sunday morning, I go into my office and I pray, 'Lord, in a few minutes I will be taking your word in my hand. And I will be sharing your word with the people who show up here today. Make me worthy to do that.' You cannot do anything at all for God unless God prepares you, unless God empowers you, unless God gives you that privilege. So the first thought that comes to your mind is before I do anything at all for God, I need to sanctify myself. Before we open our mouth to pray publicly, we need sanctification. Before we start leading the worship, we need sanctification. We do not need to put up a show. We should bring glory to God's name.

So one of the indicators of whether you are falling in line with God is how deeply you desire sanctification in your life. When you fall in line with God, the first thought that comes to your mind is I need cleansing. I need that blood of the lamb applied over me again. Otherwise I cannot stand up before God. I cannot do anything for God. And that's exactly what David did. David called the people, especially the Levites. This time it is all about the Levites because they were the ones who were assigned to carry the ark on your shoulder. This time they were going to do it right. So David asked the Levites to sanctify themselves.

Secondly, you see people giving their shoulders for the task. That's very important. You may wonder why I emphasize that. Let me make it practical. When we started our church and realized we have a lot of little kids and were looking for volunteers, some of our dear ones, well meaning folks, came to me and said, 'Pastor, we will contribute money, hire somebody to do this.' I said no and they could not understand why I said no. It was because God's work is not about money. God's work is about giving your shoulders. And when we fall in line with God, one of the fundamental changes that happen in us is that we change our attitude. And we will say, Lord, where should I give my shoulder? Show me the task. I will give my shoulder to it.

When God moves in your life, when God moves in your heart there will be a willingness to do your share. Nobody has to force you. Pastor does not have to encourage you again and again. There will be a willingness to give your shoulders to do God's work.

Thirdly, again there was singing but this time it was the Levites singing instead of the crowds shouting. Remember the first time they went to get the arc there were thirty thousand people singing. A much bigger crowd singing and playing instruments. And this time David said, no. I am a musician but I am staying back. I write the songs but I am staying back. I know how to play the harp but I am staying back because the Levites are the ones who are assigned to do it and I want them to do it. And sometimes when people come and ask me, 'Pastor, can we just put this person up there to do that ministry? What is the big deal?' The big deal is that people who have been chosen by God should do it.

In the New Testament there is a teaching on the priesthood of believers and I believe in that. Sometimes people take it to an extreme and people look down on Pastors and say what the big deal about being a Pastor is? In some churches the Pastor sits on the stage. So one day a man got up when there was a fight in his church and said, 'Pastor, there is only one difference between you and us. You are sitting this way (gesture to the pews) and we are sitting this way (gesture to the stage).' Is that true? No! If God has called you to lead the worship, you must lead the worship. If God has called you to lead the prayer, you lead the prayer. If God has called you to preach, you preach the word. It does not matter if the person sitting next to you knows the Bible more than you. Please understand that every person will be used by God somewhere, but in a given setting and in an order. God is a God of order.

Sometimes people get burned out because nobody comes to help them, nobody supports them, and nobody volunteers their time. They get tired after a while and they come to me and say, Pastor, will you please relieve me. I don't want to do this anymore.

I don't want to go up there and sing anymore. I don't want to play instruments anymore or I don't want to this ministry or that ministry anymore but I say no. You cannot get out because God has ordained you for that ministry. God has chosen you for that. If God as chosen you, you must do it or it will stay undone. This is not a people power business. This is God's business and it must be done God's way.

Fourthly, the second time the journey was marked by sacrifices. 2 Samuel 6:13 tells us that after they carried the ark on their shoulders for six steps David told them stop there. And he brought some animals and sacrificed them right there before they continued with their journey. What was the significance of that? Six was the number of human potential. So David was saying, 'we have come as far as we can with our own strength.' And I am not taking one step further without God. If I am going to take one more step I want God to come and empower us. So he marked that journey with sacrifice and moved forward. In 1 Chronicles 15, we read about the sacrifices given later by the Levites who carried the ark. When they were carrying the ark they were thinking about Uzzah. They were thinking, 'Are we any better than Uzzah? He ministered before that ark for twenty years. Yet he touched it one time and he was killed. But here we are carrying the same ark on our shoulders. How come God is not killing us? Is it because we are better than Uzzah? Is it because we are holier than him?' No, the only thing was that they sanctified themselves for the task.

Even then there is a fear of God. The fear of God is back and because of that they are praying, 'Lord, this is a mission given to us and if we can successfully carry out this mission, as soon as we get to Jerusalem the first thing that we who were part of this will get together and give a big sacrifice to honor you, Lord.' And they carried that out faithfully.

When you carry God's presence, when you are being used by God, it is so easy for us to forget after a few months where we came from and that God in His mercy is using us and start thinking that I am better than everyone else and that is why God has given me this privilege. It has absolutely nothing to do with you. He in His grace has chosen you to carry this out.

Serve the Lord with fear and bring Him honor in all occasions. And when things are done properly, and when the ministers who are doing this are under the fear of God and do things properly and give honor to God, then the dance can break out. We believe in rejoicing in the presence of God. But only after we do things properly. When you ensure that scriptural patterns are adhered to then the dance can break out. And David danced mightily.

I do not know where you are in your life today. Some of you need a new encounter with God. Let us humble ourselves before God this day.

CHAPTER XIV

Desires vs. Divine Guidance

The backdrop for this study is 2 Samuel, chapter 7, verses 17 and 18. "According to all these words and according to all this vision, so Nathan spoke to David then king David went in and sat before the Lord and He said, who am I oh Lord God? And what is my house that you have brought me this far?"

In the last chapter, we saw that finally God was bringing rest into the life of David. In fact, in Chapter 7 verse 1, starts by saying that there was rest in his life. We also saw that he became very restless because of the ark of God.

If you look at the 'rest' that came into the life of David, you can see that there was rest in four different areas. The throne was secure. Saul's family was wiped out and he did not have to worry about anyone rising up to occupy his throne. Secondly, he had a capital now. His long time dream was to secure Jerusalem as his capital. And God made that possible. Thirdly, he did not have a place to live. He was a king without a palace. But another king came forward to pay for the palace and sent the servants and workers and built a beautiful palace for him. So he had a palace of his own and a bed of his own where he could lay his head.

And finally, he was also concerned about the ark of God. He wanted to make sure that the presence of God would return to his people. Now, everything was taken care of. So now David should be resting, right? You work hard when we are young, we go to college and we graduate from college, and hopefully land a nice job, and then we try to make money and we do not want to work all our lives. But we want to work for a while and get to a point where we can start relaxing. Unfortunately, in modern day life, I don't know when people get to relax because life's challenges keep on increasing. But that's our goal. We want to get to a place where we can rest.

Now if you are in the place of David, I am pretty sure, once your capital is secure your throne is secure, your power is secure, your position is secure, you have a nice home to rest and finally you are doing something for God and God is pleased with that, then you can say maybe I can rest for a while. It did not happen. When I started reading this chapter and started writing this chapter the first thought that came to my mind was maybe David is a workaholic, like me. When you look at the background of David, it was an action filled life. Many of the actions were negative but nonetheless it was an action filled life. Somebody was always chasing him; he was always escaping from somebody, running from one cave to another. So it was a very action filled life. Maybe he missed that. Maybe he was not wired for a life of relaxation. He had to do something. Is that the story here? No, that was not it.

This restlessness was brought about by guilt. Every time David entered his palace he would see the gorgeous palace made of cedar wood and enjoyed its nice smell, when he laid down on the bed that was probably made of ivory he would feel guilty because he realized that he brought the Ark back into the city of Jerusalem but nonetheless the Ark is sitting under a little tent behind a curtain. The word for the tent that David built in the Hebrew language is Ohel, which simply means a small tent made with leather. So he probably took the camel or cow hide and just put a little curtain around the posts with the Ark underneath it.

David felt guilty about it. He said, 'this is the God who elevated me and made me worthy of this palace.' He gave me this palace, gave me this throne, gave me this position, gave me all the blessings that I enjoy today and His ark is behind a little curtain, exposed to all the elements and the severe weather in the Middle East, whereas I am enjoying my cedar palace. How was that justifiable? He decided he should do something about this. He called the prophet Nathan and asked for a word from the Lord. He expressed his desire to do something for the Lord. David did not say what he was planning to do; he just said I want to do something for the Lord because I am concerned about the Ark being exposed to all the elements. When the Ark was in the tabernacle, it was placed in the holy of holies. When you went into the tabernacle, on the outer court there were a set of curtains and then there was some space and then came the inner area and then there were curtains again and then came some space and then came the innermost part which we call the holy of holies. So even though it was behind curtains, there were three layers of curtains separated by spaces. Even when you looked upward, there were three layers of curtains. The Ark was never exposed to elements.

When the high priest went into the holy of holies, even though the tabernacle was pitched in a desert place, it was very dark inside the holy of holies because of the three layers of curtains surrounding it and the three layers of curtains above it. And nobody was allowed to light up a lamp inside the holy of holies. What provided the light for the holy of holies? The Shekinah, glory of God, a little luminous cloud that was above the Ark was what was providing the light. That was the only light that was allowed. So it was somewhat a dark place even though the tabernacle itself was pitched in a desert under severe sun. It is no wonder, David as a worshipper began to feel guilty about it. He thought this was not right. He was not doing this the right way. It is true that David brought the Ark back into the city of God but he did not put it in a tabernacle. All I did was just pitch a little tent and put the Ark there.

Look at the heart of a worshipper! Now you are a worshipper, I am a worshipper. But let me ask you how concerned are you about the presence of God? How concerned am I? Are we really particular that we must do the best for the Lord? Do you feel pressure in your heart that I must do the best for the Lord today? I know when you go to your job you feel that pressure. Monday through Friday you feel that pressure because you know there are layers of leaders above you, there are supervisors and managers and executives above you who are always looking into the quality of your work. They are always evaluating you and making little notes about you. I want to ask you when you come on Sunday morning do you feel that type of pressure? Or do you go to church with the attitude God must be pleased? God has no right to complain. At least I woke up Sunday morning. At least I showed up Sunday morning. That is better than some others, I must agree. But the heart of a true worshipper is never satisfied by giving lip service to God. The heart of a true worshipper is never satisfied by running a program on Sunday morning.

Thus, David felt guilty. He went to the prophet and said, 'Can I do something about it?' And the prophet said, 'go ahead, God is with you. Just do according to the wishes in your heart.' That is why this chapter is titled "Desire vs. Divine Guidance". This man was a true prophet. I want you to know that even a prophet can make a mistake, if he does not consult with God.

A prophet cannot prophesy all the time. In a meeting when they come, they come prepared and they spend a lot of time in prayer and they are spiritually ready to minister and they come and sometimes people won't go. Some people won't go to the front for prayer. The same thing with the alter call in a church. Even if the spirit moves through me or whoever else is ministering, only then do we call people forward to the front for an alter call and we know that the power of God is flowing there. Remember Luke 8, the power was with Jesus to heal. A minister knows when the power is flowing through him. But sometimes when we give the alter call people do not want to come because they are ashamed that other people are watching. So they wait until everyone leaves and when the Pastor is about to go into the car they run to the Pastor and ask for a prayer. Let me tell you, if a Pastor is a Pastor, he will pray but at that point it is just a routine prayer.

Nathan was a true prophet. We know that because of the prophecies that came forth from him before into the life of David. But this time Nathan made a mistake. David made a mistake and Nathan made a mistake. Both of these people knew as spiritual people that they must consult with God and seek the will of God. Even if you are a child of God you still have to seek the will of God. Do not take anything for granted. Everything that comes out of the mouth of an anointed man is not anointed. David did not consult with God. Nathan did not consult with God and Nathan was probably impressed with the way David brought the Ark to the city of Jerusalem. So he said, 'if God helped you to go this far he will help you to do the rest. So just go and do whatever is in your heart.' Big mistake!

But one good thing about this prophet was that he was an obedient prophet. It is not easy to be the national prophet of Israel and walk into the palace and say, 'hey, I made a mistake yesterday.' Because David is never alone in the palace. There are always a lot of people filling the palace. There were also hundreds of servants in the palace. So to say in front of all of them that you made a mistake is not easy. Many times people will not do that. People would rather cover up their mistake than admit their mistake. But the Bible tells us very clearly that if we cover up our mistakes God will never use us again. Do you know how many people lost their ministry because of their cover up?

But our God is a God of compassion. Psalm 100 tells us that, "He knows our nature". And if we confess our sins He is just and faithful to forgive us and restore us. So you can continue with your ministry. Nathan probably felt very bad but nonetheless he came back to David and said, 'Yesterday I made a mistake. I did not consult with God before I shared that prophesy with you. Now, this is what God is truly saying: You should not build the temple.'

God's work cannot be done according to our plans or our goals or our timetable because when God has a plan He has somebody in mind to accomplish that plan. Have you noticed that? God always accomplishes His plan through somebody. It may not be you. Whatever God wants to accomplish through you will always be accomplished through you. Just because there is a need out there it does not mean that you are the person called to do that. Just because God uses one pastor one way, it does not mean that you need to copy that person thinking that you will get a lot of popularity and you will gather a lot of following. No, it will not happen. You will end up making a fool of yourself.

Talk about good intentions! There was a time when I was involved with so many ministries because I was not good at saying no to anyone. I was involved in ministry. I did not do it for position or popularity. I was so excited, I had just started ministering and God was using me and I just wanted to be used here, used there. God said no! If we focus on what God tells us to do then we will do a good job and we will be successful. If you minister where God has placed you to minister, you will be a hero there. People will respect you and people will honor you. But when you go by your own intentions, and start ministering somewhere else where God has not called, you become a trouble for everyone. Nobody will respect you. Nobody wants to see you. It will lead to nothing but headaches. So even when you are trying to do something for God make sure God is directing your footsteps.

When David said this, he was in the prime of his youth and so used to conquering everything and he was trying to establish this on his own. Sometimes when God stops you it is not because He does not care or because He hates your ideas or your desires but because you are not ready. The next morning if David had started building the Jerusalem temple, it would have been a small temple. Because where did David come from? For many years he was struggling. He was hiding in caves. We have covered that stage in his life. Somebody else was feeding him. Remember one time, he had to go and beg for dinner from a wealthy farmer. When you are in that stage in your life, even though your desires are good, you do not have the means. You have not reached the stage in your life to do it and that is why God said no.

We can see many other reasons why God stopped David. For example, he did not know that he was about to make a historic shift in worship in Israel. In 2 Samuel chapter 7 verse 4, this is what we read: "But it happened that night that the word of the Lord came to Nathan saying, go and tell my servant David, thus says the Lord, would you build a house for me to dwell in?" Isn't that rather presumptuous! That is what God is saying. We will come to that later. "For I have not dwelt in a house since the time that I brought the children of Israel out from Egypt even to this day but have moved about in a tent and in a tabernacle." This is what God is saying: 'I never had a stationery presence in Israel. Your God was mobile, so to speak.'

If you look at Exodus, chapter 40, verse 36-37, this is what we see. It took a long time for Moses to gather everything for the tabernacle. To get people for the tabernacle and finally when he erected the tabernacle, it was not a permanent structure. This is what God told Moses, "Whenever the cloud was taken up from above the tabernacle the children of Israel would go onward with their journeys. But if the cloud was not taken up then they did not journey till the day that it was taken up." That means God took full control of the tabernacle. Moses is the one who built it but God said this is not your tabernacle. This is my tabernacle and I have no plan to stay in this location forever. God had already found a place where his temple will eventually be built. Nobody knew at that time where it was. So God told them, 'Above the tabernacle you will see the Shekinah cloud, my presence in the form of a cloud, if the cloud stays, you stay. The moment the cloud is lifted up start to get ready. Take your tents and start moving.' Immediately they had to uproot all the tents and start moving.

They were following the cloud. Wherever the cloud stopped they pitched the tabernacle, but only as long as the cloud would stay. Let us say a week later the cloud started moving again. Then, they had to uproot all the tents, pack up everything and start following the cloud again.

When we come to the book of Joshua, we see that when they entered into the Promised Land Joshua built an altar (Joshua 8:30) on Mt. Ebal and it was the mount from where all the curses were uttered (Deut. 27:11-13). Joshua built an altar there, as Moses had instructed him, because Joshua did not want anyone in the camp to be cursed. In case someone was walking under the curse of God he wanted the altar to be close to them so they could run into the presence of God and remedy themselves. That was the idea.

And when we come to 1 Samuel 1:3, we see that now the altar had shifted again. The altar was in a place called Shiloh now. That is where the high priest Eli ministered. It was also one of the places where Samuel ministered.

Then we know that the Ark was lost in the battle when Eli's sons took it into a battle with Philistines. When the Ark was lost in the battle, Samuel would go around the nation and minister in four different cities. So it was totally mobile. And when the Ark was brought back to the Philistines it was brought back into a city called Kirjath Jearim and it stayed there for a while. God's ark had been all over the place.

Now David was deciding to place God's ark in a permanent structure he wanted to build. He did not know that he was making a historic shift in worship. Just because he was a worshipper he thought that everything that comes through his mind was from God.

He allowed David to bring the Ark into Jerusalem and it stayed under a little tent. But God said, 'I'm not complaining. David, you are the one who is complaining. See I was always moved around. I always lived in tents.' His tabernacle was nothing but a tent. It had three layers but nonetheless it was just a tent. God said, 'I have no problem. I just want to be next to my people.' This is very important for us to understand. God is not looking for crystal cathedrals. I have nothing against crystal cathedrals. When you go to third world countries you will see people worshipping under a tree. And they have tremendous worship under a tree. God is not concerned about the place; God is concerned about the people who come to worship him.

And as far as New Testament believers are concerned, we know it goes even one step further because the Bible teaches us that we are the temple of God. We carry God's presence wherever we go. So we should not give much importance to the size or beauty of the place of worship.

In Deuteronomy 16:16, God told the Israelites through Moses that when they go into the promise land God will eventually choose a place where the temple would be built. There, three times a year, all the men in Israel had to come for a holy convocation. That time they were supposed to bring their tithes and their sacrifices into the temple. But Moses did not know where that place was going to be. Joshua did not know where that place was going to be. Eli did not know where that place was going to be. Even prophet Samuel did not know where that place was going to be. At this point, David also did not know the place was going to be chosen by God. So it is completely a carnal decision to make a temple for God where David wanted it. And God said, 'I am stopping you from making that mistake because I haven't told you the place for the temple.'

As I was thinking about this, I realized that I am somebody like David. Sometimes I am in a rush to do things for God. This week, I passed by a building that I really wanted to buy for our church which looked so good at that time because we were thinking so small. I stopped my car there and I said, 'thank you Lord for not giving us this place!' When God says no to you, it is not because He hates you, it is not because He is angry at you, and it is only because He has something better planned for you! But whatever He has planned will not manifest according to your timetable. That is why the Bible tells us that we need patience. And that is a very difficult thing especially for people like me who want to do everything yesterday. I get ideas and I run with it. I am sorry for talking too much about myself. But it is the truth.

Most of us would have made the wrong choices in life if God did not stop us. Maybe it was a business we wanted to enter into and God all of a sudden choked the credit line. And you start questioning God. God will say, 'No, not now because I have something better in mind for you.' So do not get angry or despondent when God says no to you.

It is possible that some of the things that you are waiting for has not manifested yet. That is why God told us through Habakkuk even if the vision tarries, just wait for it. You cannot rush the vision. You have only one choice. You have to wait for it and God said it WILL come.

The second reason why God stopped David was this. David did not have the means to carry out his plans. He was running around through the wilderness, living at the mercy of others for many years. Others were paying for him. It was true that he had a throne but the funds just started coming in. God said, 'you do not have the means for this yet.'

I think we need to hear that message in this generation. One day when I was driving I was thinking about this. In the eighties I used to read the Forbes magazine and I used to see all these ads for fancy clothes, watches and fancy cars and never once got tempted. GQ magazine was still around but GQ was only published for a certain clientele, people who could afford things. But now? Since nobody wants to wait for anything anymore, fifteen year old kids want a $300 pair of sneakers. They do not want a $40 or $50 pair of sneakers anymore. Probably fifty percent of the people on the face of the earth do not even have a pair of shoes. Yet we are not satisfied with a $50 pair of shoes. I see college kids looking through GQ magazines and ordering stuff from there. We all know some people who have gotten into some big trouble because of that. Even when we do not have the means, we want to you live like we have the means. And we eventually become so addicted to it. We only have custom tailored shirts, custom made suits etc. Why? Once you get used to a certain lifestyle, it is very difficult to go down from there.

This lesson that God taught David is a lesson that people need to learn in our generation. Three thousand years ago God told David, wait until you have the means. That is why David probably did not appreciate it at that time. Later on when he came to his senses, he wrote this in Psalm 19:13. "Keep back your servant from presumptuous sins. Let them not have dominion over me."

When we continue in that chapter we can see that even though God asked David to stop that project cold, God liked what He saw in his heart and because of that, we see in verses 9 to 16 that God gave some tremendous promises to David. God told him that, "your name will be like the name of great men on earth." David wanted to make a house for God. God said, "No, you don't make me a house; I will make you a house." What did God mean by that? Didn't he already have a palace? God said, "You have a house where you rest but this house that I will build for you is not a building but a future. I will build you a future, which means that your prosperity that you enjoy today is not a temporary prosperity. It will not be an artificial prosperity. It will not be something that is financed by plastic cards. I am going to give you the means. I am going to establish you. And once I establish you, you are going to become like one of the greatest men who ever lived on the face of the earth." We know that is exactly what God did for David.

When God calls you and me, sometimes we rush things. We do not want to wait for God's timing. Therefore we rush things and we miss the blessing. If God stopped you in some area you should be grateful. It is because God wants to lift you to greater heights. And what God brings for you and for me is greatness, not a temporary prosperity. God told David that He will guarantee him a future. That means you are not going to move at this level today and tomorrow you sink, which is what happens when we depend on the economy, when we depend on the stock market etc. But God said, "When I elevate you, you will not come crashing down later."

Remember the promise that God told Israel a long time ago? You will be the head not the tail. God did not say one day you will be the head and the next day you will be the tail. When God raises you up, you go from greatness to greatness. God said, 'I am going to build you a house.' That means you are going to have future generations who will be enjoying the greatness that you enjoy in your life.

God continued, 'I will set up your seed after you and that seed will build a house for my namesake.' In the same chapter where he stopped him telling him, 'David, I didn't tell you where you have to erect this building, don't just put this temple somewhere,' a few verses down he said,' I am going to give you a seed and I am going to let him build the temple.'

When He said that, there was a hidden promise in it. By the time he comes on the throne I will reveal to you where my temple is supposed to be. Today it is not revealed. See, God moves according to His timetable. God promised, 'I will reveal it to you and he will build the temple for me.' Then God said, 'I will not remove My mercy from him and your kingdom and your house will be established forever and your throne will be established forever.' We are waiting for the last promise. When that kingdom is established forever, we know that it will be done through the son of David Lord Jesus Christ. When He comes and He establishes that kingdom that lasts forever, we will also have a share in it.

Even when God says no, God supplants that with promises. God said no to David but then He started unrolling promises after promises. What will you go after? Your own desires? Or divine guidance in your life? Psalm 37:4 tells us that, "He shall give you the desires of your heart." And so many times we quote that verse without caring to note the first part of that verse. The first part of that verse is "Delight yourself also in the Lord." That means if you are asking things according to God's will, then He has no problem to give you the desires of your heart.

The Bible puts limits on desires. The world rouses up desires in your heart that do not necessarily coincide with godly desires. Commercials are made for that. When you watch that beer commercial, in the end you can always see somebody leaving with a girl. You may be a child of God but when you are sitting in front of that TV and you see these messages again and again, it goes into your subconscious mind. Eventually you will end up doing the same unless you put a limit to your desires. The Bible is very specific about this. Read through the book of Proverbs. In black and white it tells us so many things explicitly. If you have unbridled desires in your life and act on Sunday morning as a Christian, hoping that grace covers everything and so it does not matter, you are going to make a wreck of your life.

The only desires that God will grant us is the desires that will allow us to delight in Him. That means we are asking for His counsel. Ask anything according to the word that is revealed and it will be granted to you.

Eventually, God gave David the means. In 1 Chronicles 29: 1-9 we read, *"Further king David said to all the assembly, my son Solomon whom alone God has chosen, is young and inexperienced. And the work is great because of the temple is not for man but for the Lord God. Now for the house of my God I have prepared with my might, gold for the things to be made of gold, silver for the things of silver, bronze for the things of bronze, iron for the things of iron, wood for things of wood, onyx stones, stone to be set, glistening stones of various colors, all kinds of precious stones and marble slabs in abundance."* David, now you are ready for the temple! Twenty-four years ago when David expressed that interest in 2 Samuel 7, he had nothing. And God said, 'You don't have the means. Wait until I give you the means.' Look what happened when God gave him the means!

David said, "I have all these things in abundance, moreover because I have set my affection on the house of my God I have given to the house of my God over and above all that I have prepared for the Holy house of God, my own special treasure of gold and silver." He had accumulated three thousand talents of gold of Ophir, and seven thousand talents of refined silver, to overlay the walls of the houses. "The gold for things of gold and silver for things of silver and all kinds of work to be done by the hands of craftsmen." What is he saying? It's all from my treasure. Imagine the wealth of David by the time he died, if he could give three thousand talents of gold as a free will offering for the temple of God! If he could give seven thousand talents of refined silver, imagine the wealth. No wonder God stopped him years ago.

God may be saying no to a lot of little dreams in your life. God is challenging you to trust Him. Just go with Him. Let Him take you forward step by step. And God is challenging us and saying, see where I will take you. How strong I will make your hand.

Will you put your trust in God? Do you believe that God can take you to that height in your personal life? The God of David is your God. God of Israel is your God. And he wants to take you to places in your life. So let us give up our desires and let us seek divine guidance in our lives.

CHAPTER XV

Sowing and Reaping

In the last chapter, we were in 2 Samuel 12, learning lessons from an incident that happened in the life of David with Bathsheba. We looked at a number of factors that eventually caused the incident. We could see that there were possibilities for something like that existing in the life of David a long time before the incident actually took place. We saw that that possibility came into existence because of the compromise that David made in one area. We looked at Deuteronomy 17:16 and 17 where God had laid out three fundamental qualities for future leaders in Israel. God had expressly prohibited them from doing three things. One was accumulating money for themselves using the position of spiritual leadership. Secondly, God said, you should not accumulate horses for yourself. When you go out into the battle you should always trust in me. You should not have a lot of chariots and horses. And the third thing that God prevented the leader from doing is multiplying wives.

We saw in our studies that David had absolutely no problem in taking care of two of the three parts that God demanded from him. When he won battles and there were Arabian horses in those battles, without any mercy he killed every one of them because he remembered what God asked of a leader in Israel. He had no problem killing precious animals. And then we also saw that all the bounty that he got from these battles, he kept it aside for the temple and he never took a penny from it for himself. David kept the promise in that area as well, where God said a leader should not increase wealth for himself using the victories I give. So he had no problem there. But in the third area he compromised God's command. We saw in 2 Samuel 5, that as soon as he became king, one of the first things that he did was take multiple wives and concubines for himself and that is where the whole problem started.

Many times when we have failures in our life we only look at that moment as if that moment exists by itself. But nothing exists by itself. It is always a series of incidents that lead to a failure in a leader's life.

The reason for summarizing the three demands is this. Our meditations for this chapter begin there. When Nathan came back to David and told him that he did something extremely unpleasant in the sight of God because not only had he taken Bathsheba as his wife but also killed her husband in that process. He became a murderer. God said, 'you are a person who is supposed to know me. You say you are a person who knows me and worships me. And I said about you that you are a person after my own heart. When we have that kind of relationship between you and Me, you cannot do these kind of things and get away with it. I will forgive you but you still have to bear the consequences of sin.'

In 2 Samuel 12:10, Nathan told David, 'Because you have done this and brought shame to the name of your God, the sword shall never depart your home.' Every time something wrong happens in our life, every time we get caught up in sin, it is like we are sowing a seed of something. God has built a system into the universe: Every time you sow something you will eventually reap a harvest of what you have sown. Even God cannot change that, it is built into the universe. That is the way God designed this universe. So every time you do something good you will reap according to that. Every time you do something bad you will reap according it and you cannot escape from it.

That does not mean that your sin is held onto you or accounted against you forever. God will forgive that sin but still you have to reap the consequences. This is something we see all around us. People do not understand this. People sometimes think if I was a smoker but then I got saved, I should not get sick. Unfortunately, it does not work that way. If you used to smoke a pack or more of cigarettes for fifteen to twenty years and then you got saved, but later on you get lung cancer, do not blame God for it because you sowed the seed for it. You are just reaping the harvest of what you sowed years ago. People live promiscuous lives for years and after awhile they get STDs and they begin to wonder how did I get sick if I am a child of God now? Well, you sowed the seeds for it. That is why the Bible tells us that we must serve the Lord with fear. We cannot take liberty with our lives. We cannot compromise in areas of life and then expect God to whitewash all of that.

That is the difference between a child of God and a person who did not know God. You may ask me, 'Pastor, if I become a child of God what is the difference between me and a man or woman in the world, if both of us will reap the results of what we sow?' The difference is that you may reap the harvest, but in the midst of that you will see the grace of God reaching out to you. You will see the Holy Spirit ministering to you. You will see the Holy Spirit giving you the strength and stamina to overcome the challenges. Even if it leads eventually to your death, there will be an unshakable peace in your life, since your eternity is secure.

God sent prophet Nathan and gave a long list of promises to David's household. Incredible promises had been given to him but then David messed up. It is not God who messed up, David messed up. God was in a dilemma now. He had to keep His word. He told David that after him, his son would sit on the throne, and that from generation to generation this throne would belong to his home. God said, 'I promised you that I will be like a father to your children. Even when they go wrong I will punish them with a stick of man. I am going to use only human standards to punish them and not eternally punish them.' And God gave them all those promises on one side but now that David had done this, He had to address this as well. So God said, 'from one side the blessings will come from the other side the sword will come.' So both the blessings and the sword met together in the household of David as we see in 2 Samuel, chapter thirteen.

From chapter thirteen through eighteen is a very sad passage in the pages of the Bible. The house of a worshiper was in turmoil, the house of a godly man was in turmoil, the house of a man who had victories in the name of God was in turmoil. Don't we see that around us today? How many cases like that do we see in the world in which we live today? Not because of God, God wants it to be only blessings. God expects us to go straight forward like an arrow and keep receiving the blessings into our lives but then we interject something into the picture and mess up the picture. So on one side the blessing is coming and on the other side the punishment is coming. On one side you have the presence of God, you have the joy of salvation, you have the presence of the Holy Spirit in your life but on the other side you can see the judgment coming. God start touching you adversely here and there. That is not the way God expects us to live. If it is our life story we cannot blame God, it's our doing. Same thing was unfolding in the household of David.

David was a man who could rule a country but who could not rule his household. Is that possible? Yes, it is possible. Two years ago, when I was coming back from a mission trip overseas, I saw a movie on the flight. The title of the movie was "My Father the Mahatma". It was the life story of the son of Mahatma Gandhi made into a movie. I was crying by the time that movie was over because this man was so messed up. You would not expect Mahatma Gandhi's son to be so messed up. We put Mahatma Gandhi on a pedestal. But his son was totally confused and died on a street one day. This proves it is possible to be the United States president and not have your household in order. It is possible for you to be the denominational head leading ten thousand churches and still not have your house in order. You see, we need God at every stage of our life.

Remember how David was always trusting in God even for little things? We saw him at different junctures of his life, going to God and asking His counsel and making sure that every step he took was according to the counsel of God. So God kept elevating him. Then one day all of a sudden he felt like us and said, 'I have arrived; now I can take care of myself, I don't have to ask God.' It resulted in one mistake in his life. And guess what? His life started going down. This incident was a one-time incident. David didn't go after lady after lady. It was only a one-time incident. But by the time David did this, he was a middle aged man. He had adult children growing up in his house who were watching all of this. Then God decided to pop the lid on this incident and make it public. So the whole country came to know about it. His ministers came to know about it. His generals came to know about it.

In that process he lost the moral authority that he enjoyed all along. In David's life the throne was not the big thing. He was always a godly leader. For many years he was in a cave but he had moral authority over his people. You see, it is not the throne that matters, it is not the title that matters. It is your relationship with God that really matters. You can live in a cave and be a very strong godly leader. And you can have a most luxurious palace and have no moral authority at all. So we have to choose how we will live.

And when we come to chapter 13 and 14, we see a dark saga opening up in the house of David because his children started playing a very deadly game. David had many wives and many concubines. So, many half brothers and half sisters were growing up under one roof. And they all started flirting with each other and then it led to the rape of a young girl. The Bible shows the name of at least eighteen sons that David had but only one daughter. So you can imagine how precious that little girl was. But that one girl that David had, got raped when she was young and never got married for the rest of her life. So you can imagine the darkness that was coming into that home because of the father's sin, not because of anything that the kid did.

The kids started taking liberties because now the father did not have the authority to stop them. We as fathers have God given authority. But we only have that authority as long as we live a godly life. The moment we stop living that godly life, the moment that our children find out that, their father is a sham and this whole thing is a show and dad does not live a godly life, our moral authority is gone. Once our moral authority is gone our children start to rebel and all of a sudden you will see things change in your home. And that is exactly what happened in David's home.

The children started taking advantage of the situation. Then, another son of David, Absalom, who was the most handsome among all of David's sons, fell victim to ungodly behavior because of his father's indiscretion in handling his sister's rape case. He was a loving kid but all of a sudden, he started rebelling. Three chapters in this story are completely dedicated to this young man because he was completely lost. This is a kid who the father is expecting to become the future king. But the father is not in a position to nurture him to that level.

How many of us have sons growing up in our homes? We have a God given responsibility to lead them to adulthood. We have a God given responsibility to place them in a position of authority, a position of prominence, something better than what we had. That is why God placed us on earth as fathers. Not to preside over the funerals of our sons. Not to sit down in a corner and cry about our sons who are no longer there. God placed us on earth to be a guiding force in their lives and start impacting their lives beginning in early childhood. Bring them up right and by the time they become adults they know how to handle all the challenges in life. It is then that we can step aside and leave them at the forefront. That is what God expects from us. But David did not have that good fortune. David was a great ruler, a great worshipper, wrote a lot of Psalms but was a failure as a father. In fact, he presided over the funeral of at least three of his sons before he himself passed away.

What happens when you create a crisis in your life? It was not a God given crisis. It was not even Satan. Let me show you what is going to happen when we create crisis for ourselves. First of all, people will always recognize your weakness. Even in nature we see that wherever there is weakness others can sense it. Have you noticed preying animals when they are chasing a whole herd of animals they are always looking for the weakest one because they know there is no point in going after the strong one? So the moment you create a weakness in your life, the enemy picks that up. And the enemy makes provisions to take maximum advantage of your weakness. In David's case, his own children took advantage of it. David could not stop them and we can see up to 2 Samuel 18 that dark story continues.

The second thing is this: When there is a crisis in your life, somebody will always try to make a profit out of it. Let me give you a number of examples from this passage. First of all, we see a man named Ahithophel in 2 samuel15. The Bible tells us that this was a wise man; that his counsel was the counsel from God for David and even for his rebellious son Absalom because he was highly respected. He used to give counsel to David for a long time and all of a sudden we see Ahithophel joining with Absalom. Ahithopel started giving advice to Absalom. So what is Ahithophel doing? He is trying to profit out of the crisis that has come in the life of David. Do you know why? Ahithophel happened to be the grandfather of Bathsheba. I used to wonder why did this man change sides? Because he was the counselor to David for a long time and David respected him a lot but the moment a crisis came we see he is switching sides and joining with David's rebellious son. I was surprised to find out that Bathsheba was Ahithophel's granddaughter. Bathsheba's father Eliam (2 Samuel 11:3), was the son of Ahithophel (2 Samuel 23:34).

The Bible tells us that we must not let any roots of bitterness grow. The Bible advices us if something happens take care of it immediately. Do not let the sun set on it. Otherwise, the roots of bitterness will grow and eventually create problems. Ahithophel could not do anything when David violated his granddaughter because he was one of the counselors to David. But he kept that in his heart and was waiting for an opportunity to take revenge on David. When David ended up running from the kingdom because of Absalom, he knew his chance had come.

We cannot see the heart of people. People may look at you and smile broadly but you do not know what is going through their heart. If you have done something wrong to somebody you better get right with them because they are just waiting for a chance. They may even be in your church. They may give you a bear hug but watch out if there is bitterness in their heart, one day it will come out. This elderly man Ahithophel got his chance to get even with David, when David was running away from Absalom.

The second character we see in the story is a man named, Mephibosheth. Do you remember him? He was the lame son of Jonathan. And when we were talking about the covenant that David entered with Jonathan, we saw the details about Mephibosheth. When David sent people and brought him back and gave him a seat at the royal table, he was so humble and gracious. Remember the language that Mephibosheth used at that time? He said, *"What is your servant, that you should regard a dead dog like me?"* (2 Samuel 9:8). David replied because I entered into a covenant with your father. And Mephibosheth was eating from David's table for years but as soon as David got in trouble he turned against David. In 2 Samuel 16, he told his servant that today the kingdom is going to come back to the household of Saul. 'Israel is going to make me the next king.'

This man did something totally foolish because he was in no position to oppose David. In 2 Samuel, chapter 9, verse 9, when David originally brought him to the table, David not only gave him a seat at the table but David gave him also all the land that belonged to his father. King Saul came from a very wealthy family. All the land that belonged to his family was given back to Mephibosheth. But because of Mephibosheth's efforts to take advantage of David's crisis, David took all the land away from him and gave it to his servant Ziba (2 Samuel 16:4).

Again in 2 Samuel 16, we see is a man called Shimei. This man belonged to the household of Saul. For almost two decades, there were battles between these two houses (2 Samuel 2). And the household of David was going up and the household of Saul was coming down. But nonetheless, in the end there were a few people left in the household of Saul. Shimei was one of them. He is another guy who was really resentful. Not everyone enjoys your success in life. When God blesses you, do not make the mistake of thinking that everyone is going to be a cheerleader for you. A lot of people will resent you for your blessings. A lot of people will resent you for God's presence in your life. When they see they are going down and you are going up, they take note of it and they become resentful. When you keep going up, they cannot do anything to you because God is on your side, people are on your side and blessings are on your side. But should you stumble one day, should you do something dumb in your life one day, all these people who were resenting you for all these years will all of a sudden show up. And that is the story of Shimei.

Shimei was watching David since he started out as the little shepherd boy. Then God elevated him and he became a great king in that generation. Was he resenting David? All this used to belong to his family. His uncle Saul's son should have been sitting on the throne. But he kept quiet, kept a low profile until he got a chance. Be watchful in life. That is why the Bible tells us, as much as possible, try to live in peace with everyone. Because when you have enemies they are always on the lookout for you. They are waiting for the moment you stumble in your life; to get you; to pull you down. Shimei showed up just as David was crying because his own son initiated this rebellion and he was running away from the kingdom. And while he was crying all the people with him were crying. Suddenly they heard someone cursing at the top of his lungs. That was Shimei. He said, 'You are a bloodthirsty man. The throne belongs to our family; the throne belongs to our uncle Saul. You took it away from him. And today God is judging you for that. God is punishing you for that.' Well? We could live with that assessment if it was true.

We have seen that David did not move a finger to get the throne. Even when the throne was his to take, he stayed away from king Saul and never did him any harm. He waited and waited, suffered indignities, suffered treachery, suffered poverty and was sleeping in caves even though he knew he was anointed to be the king. He never went after it until God put it into his lap one day. Until king Saul was removed from the scene in a battle.

But Saul's family did not look at it that way. You may look at things one way and your enemies will always look at things in a different way. You have one set of explanation for whatever is going on and your enemies, people who resent you, have a completely different explanation for what is happening in your life. You may truthfully say that this is God's doing, I do not know what is going on in my life. I do not know why all these things are happening in my life. Or you may agree that you did something wrong and you are suffering for it. You may be confident that

God will restore you. Your enemy does not look at it that way. The enemy will see this as the opportunity to finish you off. Shimei said, 'my uncle cursed you before he died. At this point, all the curses are coming upon you. That is why you are going through this.'

This was a wrong assessment because David did nothing to get the curses from king Saul. He always treated king Saul with respect. Whatever David was going through in his life at that particular junction was his own making. When you go through situations, many times people do not understand why. Everyone has an explanation for you. When Job and his family were going through severe trials, it happened because of a wager between God and Satan and the family of Job just became the pawn in that game. But everyone who showed up in Job's home had a completely different explanation. Everyone wanted Job to confess his sins. He must have done something wrong to go through this. Job said, 'I don't know. I don't know what I did. All I know is that I tried my best to please God.' But his friends would come back again and say no you are pretending to be a saint but you are a sinner and that is why you are going through this.

The world becomes a cruel place when you go through problems. You will seldom see somebody who understands you. You seldom see somebody who will sympathize with you. But you find a lot of people who want to jump on you in that weak moment in your life and try to finish you off. And that is exactly what Shimei did.

The fourth character we see is a character called Joab. And he was one of the generals of David. He also took matters into his own hand. He killed Absalom, the son who initiated this rebellion. One would think it was a good thing. Initially it may look like that. But it is not because Joab never had the full trust of king David. Initially he was supporting king Saul and he was a general for king Saul. When king Saul was defeated he changed sides and came to the side of king David. So King David and his generals always looked at him suspiciously. He was taking advantage of the situation. What was his motive? He wanted to get on the good side of the king. He thought if he killed Absalom, the king would support him fully. Wrong assessment! King David had told him specifically to show mercy to his son.

There are spiritual lessons in all of this. The Bible tells us that Satan is running around looking for whosoever he may devour. Satan had his eyes upon you a number of times. But God said, 'He is struggling but he is My son. He is going through problems but he is My son. He is caught up in bad habits but he is My son. I know he is not doing very well but he is My son. I want you to treat him as my son.' That is why we are here today. There is a heavenly king who also happens to be your heavenly Father. And He shows mercy unto you and me. The Bible tells us He pities his children. Do you see the difference between God and people?

Remember the principle that we are establishing through this study: You will always reap what you sow. Joab thought that he would get on the good side of the king and probably become the four star general in David's army by doing this but that is not what happened. Eventually we know that Joab was killed. So we will always end up paying for what we do.

There is a fifth man we see in this story is named Bursillai. He was not even a Jewish man. He was a gentile person from Gilead. And we see that he was a wealthy man and when the king was running away and was in a foreign country, everyday he would send food for David and for all who were in his company from his house. Bursillai was a very caring fatherly figure to David. Later on when Solomon became the king, one of the last pieces of advice that David gave to Solomon was make sure you take care of the household of Bursillai (1 King 2:7). He said, let his sons come and eat at your table. They were already wealthy but now they became royalty. The Bible tells us that our God is not an unjust God. "For God is not unjust to forget your work and labor of love which you have shown toward His name, in that you have ministered to the saints, and do minister." (Hebrews 6:10). Jesus said, if you give even a glass of water in His name you will always get a reward for it (Mathew 10:42).

You have two ways to look at people who are struggling. When you are going through struggles, you can walk away as we read many did in the story of the Good Samaritan. Or you can make up your mind to go and help that person. But in the process of helping that person, you do not know what is going to happen to you later in life. You may only show a little mercy to somebody but it will come back a hundred fold into your life and into your children's life. Bursillai never expected anything in return because he was well off already. He knew the king was in trouble. And for some reason he liked David so he kept on sending food. And when he did that, he never expected that his sons would be sitting at the royal table one day. And that is the same promise that God gives us. When we do something for God, God will reward us. It is guaranteed.

The crisis in David's life went on for a while and we know how it ended. Joab didn't show mercy to Absalom. Even though the king said to show mercy to his son, he did not. He and his cohorts stood around Absalom while he was hanging from a tree. While he was helpless, he thrust a spear through his heart. He was not satisfied with that so they beat him up like a dog until he died. The king heard about it and mourned for his son. Eventually the crisis was over.

There are some spiritual lessons in the story of David's return to the throne at the end of this story. First of all there is a tremendous parallel to our expectant waiting of our king Lord Jesus in this passage. In 2 Samuel 19:9 and 10, we read, "And all the tribes were in a dispute throughout all the tribes of Israel, saying, the king saved us from the hand of our enemy, he delivered us from the hand of the Philistines; and now he has fled from the land because of Absalom." "And Absalom, who we anointed over us, died in battle. Now therefore, why do you say nothing about bringing back the king?" When David was ruling on that throne Israel was a great nation. Israel had prospered. Everyone was looking at them with respect and everything was going smoothly. The moment David left the throne the whole country came into disarray. Everything was going wrong in the country. Now this is interesting, listen to what the people were saying. 'We let David go.' These are the same people who joined with Absalom.

When I look at this picture, I see a close parallel to what happens to the world in the absence of Jesus. Two thousand years ago when Jesus was walking on earth, he was healing the sick, restoring people, bringing the dead back to life. Everything was going well. But then, they rejected Jesus just like they rejected David and preferred Absalom. Remember when they rejected Jesus and said they want Barabbas? But look at the world today after rejecting Jesus for the last two thousand years, we see nothing but battles and famine and issues and pestilence and plagues and nothing but bad stories. We live in a day where calamities are increasing and the peace is departing from the world. People are living in total confusion.

And now the people are saying we need the king back because the country is in disarray. The country has no peace, no administration, no blessings; everything is gone so we need the king back. In 2 Samuel 19:12, you see a plea from king David to the people of Judah. "You are my brethren. You are my bone and my flesh; then why are you the last to bring back the king?" David was pleading to his own tribe. And that is a challenge to us as believers.

Today the focus has shifted in preaching. When I was young I used to listen to message after message about the second coming of Jesus Christ and now, very few talk about the second coming of Jesus Christ. Majority is talking about prosperity and cars and mansions and jet planes and everything else in this world. But hardly anyone speaks about the second coming. When we went for conventions years ago, it was guaranteed that the Saturday night speaker, whoever it was, would be speaking about the second coming of Jesus Christ. But today nobody does that. The church is more interested in THIS world. Our king, the son of David, Lord Jesus Christ is making that same plea to you and me today. He is saying, 'you are my bone and you are my flesh. How come you are the last to bring the king back?'

How many of us are really interested in the return of Jesus? You may say, 'Pastor, not now! Tell Him to wait for ten more years. I just started my life. Let me enjoy my life a little.' This is the problem with that answer: In ten years another generation comes up with that same answer. We just started our life, and it goes on.

The Bible tells us that we have a role to play in bringing king Jesus back to earth. Do you know that? The return of Jesus

Christ is also dependent on you. I know Jesus said, when my Father tells me to go I will go but it is also dependent on you. He said very clearly in the gospel of Matthew that "And this gospel of the kingdom will be preached in all the world as a witness to all the nations, and then the end will come." (Mathew 24:14). If you do not take the gospel to others, we are delaying the second coming of Jesus.

Sometimes people ask me, 'Pastor, why do you go abroad? Why do you like to go on mission trips so much?' Pastors whom we help have told me that this is the very first time in the history of these tribes that they are hearing about Jesus Christ. Do you know how many tribes are still left in the world who have never heard about Jesus? When Jesus said, this gospel shall be preached to all the nations, the Bible meant all the people groups. They also need to hear the gospel. Only then shall the end come.

Do you know why? Because there is a great promise in Revelations 5, when we get to Heaven and we sing the song of salvation it says there that there will be at least one person from every people group on the face of the earth in Heaven. How can they hear if someone is not sent? That is why we get involved in missions. That is why we preach the gospel. That is why share the gospel. How many people have you shared the gospel with? Have you led at least one person to Christ in your life? When you get to heaven there should be at least one person who will stand up and say, 'Lord Jesus I am here because of this man; because of this sister who shared the gospel with me.' If you do not share the gospel with others, you are delaying the coming of Jesus.

We saw that David got the heart of the people united. He stayed on the other side of the Jordan until all the people were ready. Verse 14 of that chapter tells us that 'the entire people were ready as one man' and then they sent for David and he came back. The Bible tells us that that is when Jesus is also going to come back. "And the spirit and the bride say "Come!" And let him who hears say, "Come! And let him who thirsts come. Whosoever desires, let him take the water of life freely." (Revelation 22:17)

How many of you are ready to shout, 'come Lord Jesus quickly?' We should not be surprised when He comes back. He comes back for only two things. First, there is a group that is waiting for him and he is coming to receive them unto him. And then there is a group who is not ready for him. The moment he returns, the world enters into judgment. So are you ready to invite Jesus back? Are you ready to shout come Lord Jesus quickly? If you are ready He will listen to your prayers. But if you're not ready, He is not going to write you off. Even at this moment the rivers of living waters are flowing. You can drink from it and quench your spiritual thirst. That means you can get right with God still. And you can join with the group that is ready to receive Jesus back.

Chapter XVI

Struggles of a Father

When we study the Bible we see many godly men who failed in the art of fathering. So that is something we are going to look at in the life of David. I know all the children expect their parents to be perfect and they think they are perfect when they are small. But when they grow up they realize that my father and my mother were not as perfect as I thought at one time. So that creates an issue in their lives. Sometimes they rebel, sometimes they walk away from faith because of it, though many times God in his faithfulness bring them back.

I myself being a father, this study hits very close to home. I am a father who also struggled many times. Many years I struggled. It took me a while to get a grip on fatherhood. Just because I am a pastor doesn't mean that I didn't go through any struggles or I've been a perfect person. When I got married 34 years ago, I wish there was somebody to share the message that I am sharing with you. I wish I heard a message on fatherhood in my church that I was attending. All the message I heard in those days were either legalistic dos and don'ts or the message was on the second coming of Jesus Christ. We also are living in that hope but at the same time, we must be prepared for this life here and now because we need to overcome the issues that we face today.

Our study starts in 2 Samuel13 and the main portion of this message and ends in 2 Samuel18. In the first chapter we looked at David's background. When God came into David's life and immediately we notice something that tells us something about David's childhood. That is where will start. Because as a man who is over 50 years old, I have learned one thing in my life's journey. The most important period in a person's life is his or her childhood. The things that you go through as a child does not seem big when you are a child but it becomes bigger when you are an adult. Many adults are struggling in the world today. Look at our communities, we see so many fathers who do not know how to be a father. We see so many people who do not know how to shoulder the responsibility of being an adult. And many of them are desperate. I have spent some time counseling people. From listening to life stories of people, from what they have told me, I can see that much of it comes from their childhood.

When we look at David's life and the struggles that he faced as an adult at least one of the main factors that caused it was an insecure childhood. As soon as we started the story of David, the first incident that we saw was Samuel coming to David's home with this divine mission. God is saying that I have found a new King in this home and I just want to find out who is that person. He came with anointing oil in a ram's horn which he was going to pour on the individual whom God had chosen. When the father heard that news he got very excited and invited all his children to come and to stand in front of Samuel in line so that God can show who is the person He chose. But in that process we saw that Jesse, David's father, invited the first seven sons. Even though David was the youngest, he was never invited for that special dinner. This is the most honorable moment in that family's history up to that time. Later there would be a greater honor when David became King. But imagine this is the most honorable moment in your home. But David's family did not invite him for the dinner. If you are the baby of the house, your father treating you like that is a mystery. Some people say because that David was not actually from the same mother. Maybe he was from a second mother or a concubine and that is why the father treated him that way. There is no proof for that in the Bible but that is a modern interpretation of the story.

You can see a justification for that argument later after he got the anointing and when he went into the battlefield. When all his brothers were shying away from Goliath, here is young David coming forward because of the anointing upon his life. He says, 'I can take this guy on and I will have victory for us.' But instead of appreciating him, we see the tremendous verbal abuse that he had to suffer that day from his brothers. So that also makes you wonder. Maybe he was not their blood brother. Otherwise they would not treat him that way. Either way, one thing is for sure, he did not have a very good childhood. He was never fully assimilated into his family. He had a very insecure childhood and you can see that showing up again and again in his life later. The problem with an insecure childhood is this, when you go through a lot of issues it leaves a little scar on you here and there. And you are in a rush to grow up so you don't pay much attention to it at that time. You go out, play with friends, go to school, study etc. But later on when you become an adult and you have a little more time to reflect on things, all those old scars become more and more painful in your life. If you do not know how to deal with that pain, it starts a cycle of dysfunction. And you begin to wonder what happened. I did not look at life this way. Something has happened to me and I look at myself differently now.

The problem is this. You are already an adult and married and you have started a family. If you start that married life with unresolved dysfunction in your life, you feel that you do not know how to be a husband, you do not know how to be a wife. Even though you are not saying anything in the back of your mind you are absorbed in self pity. Why did it happen to me? How am I supposed to handle this? What am I supposed to do with the life now? So that burden is always in the back of your mind and it shadows everything that you do. The cycle of dysfunction will continue in your family. When your children are born, all they see is a dysfunctional family. So when they see something portrayed by their parents, they naturally think this is the norm. All the families should be like this. They haven't seen any better than that. If my family is dysfunctional, all the families in the world should be dysfunctional. If my parents are dysfunctional that means all the parents are dysfunctional. So the children grow up thinking that this is normal and they start acting out.

When they go to school, a big surprise is waiting for everyone. They go to school and they start acting out and all of a sudden you are called into the principal's office and there are complaints from the teachers of this and that and the cycle continues. If you do not know how to deal with it, eventually it can create big problems for everyone involved in it.

That is exactly what happened in David's life. When David became an adult we see that many issues came into his life. One of these areas was marrying multiple wives. It was allowed at that time, especially he being a King. There is a problem with being a King. When you have victories and your country is expanding, the King in the neighborhood gets very concerned about it. He is afraid that you may lay eyes upon his kingdom next. In order to prevent the King from attacking his kingdom, the King would take one of his daughters to this successful King's palace and say, 'God is blessing you. You are going up and I see your kingdom is expanding and we also want to rejoice with you therefore I want to give my daughter as a wife to you.' It is actually a political move because when he gives the daughter to this King, he becomes the son-in-law, whether he wants it or not. One King is making sure that the other King will not come and attack his kingdom. Now another King hears about it and say, 'ah hah, that's wise. Let me do the same thing.' So before you know in the old days Kings ended up with multiple wives. And then they were allowed to have concubines. It becomes a big household; they call it harems in the Middle East.

When you have a situation like that, eventually boundaries become gray. If you have two children from wife #1, three children from wife #2, four children from wife #3 etc. what is the relationship between these children? Sometimes they may not even look at each other as siblings. Sometimes they may look at them as cousins. In the Jewish society, not only in the old days even now they are allowed to marry their cousins if they want.

We can see in the household of David the boundaries began to disappear and a descent started to happen in his family structure. Are these my siblings? Should I treat them as my siblings or should I treat them as my cousins? If they are my cousins then I can have a relationship with them. I can have one of them as my wife. So the graying of the boundary started creating problems in David's home.

Secondly, problems began to multiply in the life of David after the incident in 2 Samuel 12. In the previous chapter, the story is David's affair with Bethsheba. That whole incident happened because of some people's good will. David was in many battles for many years and he was getting battle fatigued and somebody and almost killed David once. So all the soldiers came to David and said please don't come to battle anymore because we want you to live for a long time. Just take care of yourself we will go and do all the battles for you. Just relax and stay at home. So instead of his regular routine and being part of a battle in that particular time when all the soldiers were in battle, David was alone at home. David was bored and pacing back and forth on the palace stoop. If you have been in the Middle East you can see that all the houses used to be next to each other, like the row houses in this country. Most of the houses are attached homes. And you can see so many homes if you look from the top of one particular home. And when David was looking, just closely looking at his kingdom, and just pacing back and forth, one beautiful lady came in his line of vision. Her name was Bethsheba. One look and David wanted her. David asked somebody to find out who she is and when the girl found out that the King is showing interest in me she fell for him. So without going through details, since we know the story, she ended up in David's palace. David ended up having a one-time affair with her and then sent her back.

So she went back home and David thought everything is hush hush. Only I know this besides my faithful servant. So it will always stay under the rug. I don't have to worry about this. But guess what, when you are a child of God, God does not allow you that break. Probably all other Kings did the same thing. We recently read about a King in one of the African nations who was taking all the teenage girls to be his wives and the Kingdom revolted against that. It came all the way to the United Nations. The King had the freedom to do that, since he was the supreme authority but when you are a child of God, you cannot take that liberty. So even though David said nobody knows this, just me and my servant, he is a very faithful servant and he would never tell anyone . . . . God saw that. God saw that and God said, no, no you cannot do that.

See the problem in getting into wrong things is this: when you do one thing wrong, in order to cover the thing that, you may end up doing more things. You only have two choices. You can confess and get right with people and God. That is the right thing to do. Many people end up using the second choice which is in their efforts to protect their honor they will try to cover it up by doing more bad things. So here was this affair and David thought it was quiet, everything is hush and then a month later Bethsheba sent the word, 'by the way I know it was only a one night stand but I am pregnant. And I know you are the father because my husband was in battle when this incident happened. So I know you are the father. I know you are the King but take responsibility for this.'

Now David is in a jam, what is he supposed to do? And David did not want anyone to know because he has an image to protect. What is the image? He has the image of a godly man. Here is a man who wrote their worship songs. It does not mean that the songs were not right. It does not mean that the songs did not come from his heart. Anyone can have a weak moment in their life. And here he is caught up in that weak moment and now it has become a big issue and he does not know how to handle it. When you do not seek the counsel of God, you end up doing the stupidest things in your life. Since all of us make mistakes in our lives, at that moment what God expects us to do is to be upfront with it, confess it and accept I made a mistake. I never thought I would do that but I did anyway. Seek forgiveness and you will be pardoned. The Bible says if you ask, God will abundantly pardon and then you can move on with your life.

But instead of doing that David got scared. 'Oh my God, what if people find out. I have this image to protect, I am supposed to be this very godly person.' When they went to tabernacle for worship service all the songs that they were singing were written by David. He is thinking, 'And then I ended up doing this. How am I going to face the people if they find out. I have to find a way to hush this down.' So he started scheming now. When you start scheming, you are no longer thinking as a child of God you have reverted back to your carnality. Your flesh has taken over. So David said, 'I know I'm the father but I have to find a way to pin this on her husband.' He checked and found out that the husband was a Captain in the army. So David said, 'I am going to send somebody to ask the guy to come home and say you have been a very faithful servant, you have been very faithful in all these battles, you do not have to fight this battle, go and spend time with your wife.' What is David thinking? Maybe that a couple of months later when it begins to show he can say it is his child? He is trying to save his face.

But this man was a genuine soldier. He said, 'No, there is no way I can go home and sleep with my wife when all my friends are in the battlefield and their wives are alone at home. I am a true soldier, I am not going to do that.' So he refused to go and the King said, 'I am going to give you a couple of blankets. Take this and go for a picnic with your wife.' The guy said, no I don't want to go for a picnic. The King said, 'I will give you the key for my rooms in the resort' and the guy said I don't want to go to the resort. Then the King realized that he is in big trouble. So he started scheming further. He told his servants to booze him up. Give him the strongest liquor in the land and then carry him and put him in his bed. So maybe this way I can later pin this on him. Can you imagine a godly man doing this? David, who wrote half of the Psalms in the Bible, doing that? He is the King so whatever the King says goes. So the servants boozed him up and said to him go and spend time with your wife. But the guy said no. They took him home and came back and the next morning they woke up and found the guy sleeping at the door of the King's palace. He said no, I will not sleep with my wife while my friends are in battlefield. What a true soldier! What a big problem for David now.

Finally David realized, there is nothing I can do, this guy is trouble. How can you go to his own soldier and confess? He could not. So he started scheming further and told his general we are in the middle of a battle, where the battle is the fiercest, take this guy and leave him there and let him be killed in the battle.

Others just back off. He would not know that he would be killed in the battle. And that is exactly what happened. This man, this perfect gentleman was killed in that battle to cover up the sin of the so called godly man. God said, 'No way! I can understand you making a mistake, anyone can make a mistake, but when you start scheming and when you start covering up and when you lead that to bloodshed, now you are a murderer. The same prophet who came to David early and gave tremendous promises for his family was summoned by God to confront David. He came back to David's home and said you are a murderer and God will deal with you as a murderer.

I want to give you two principles from here. First of all, making a mistake is natural. All of us have made mistakes in our lives including me. But if you have made mistakes in your life, the best thing that you can do for yourself and for others is to confess it. Confess it to people, confess it to God. Confess it to the person to whom you did wrong. And say, I made this mistake. I never thought I would do it but I did it. But I do not want to throw away my life because of this mistake that happened in my life. I still want to go forward and go to the destiny that God has in store for me so I seek your forgiveness. And if you are earnest, I am pretty sure that person will forgive you and you can move on in life. That's the best thing for everyone's sake so that all can move on.

Second principle is this, please do not try to cover up because you cannot cover up anything before God. The Bible tells us that everything lays before him bare and naked. God can see the deepest thoughts in our hearts. So there is absolutely no point in trying to cover anything up before God. You are wasting your time. Somebody said, you can fool some of the people all the time, all the people for some time, but you can never fool all the people all of the time. Jesus put that in a different way. He said, 'whatever is done in the closet will be shouted from the rooftop.' Jesus was saying that eventually everything is going to come out, so address it and move on in life.

God had already told David that a lot of blessings were coming to his home. He said, 'I am going to bless you, I am going to bless your children, bless your children's children. The good thing about God is, when God promises something He will carry it out. Even when we are not worthy of it anymore. So the blessing was coming from one side. But now that David has done this extremely wicked thing, and has become a murderer, God has to deal with that also, because He is a righteous judge. From one side blessings are coming, from the other side a sword is coming. And that is exactly what happened in David's family. Before David himself died at a ripe old age, four of his children were killed. He had to attend the funeral of four children at four different times because of this wickedness that he did in his life.

When God starts extracting payment from us I do not think any of us can take it. That is why the Bible says, 'Today is the day of grace. Today is the acceptable time.' Before that judgment comes get right with God. Confess your faults with God and ask forgiveness from Him because if He starts extracting payments from you, you do not have enough to pay Him back. It will be extremely difficult for us to stand before Him and give an account. So use this opportunity that God has given in your life to get right with God, if you need to.

The fourth thing I want to show you about fatherhood is this. When God himself sent a prophet and revealed everything and later wrote it in the pages of the Bible and everything became public, a whole lot of children, were watching this. David had multiple wives and a whole bunch of children are growing up in that palace. Until that day they had one view about their father. Our dad is the godliest man on earth. Look at our dad he is writing all the songs to sing in our temple. Look at our father, he is playing the instrument and playing for the glory of God. And then this news comes out. How would David's children look at their father the next day? Think about the shock of the children. Even before the children reacted in any way, as soon as this news came out, he lost the moral authority in the house.

Once you lose the moral authority in your house, disciplining your children become impossible. Because the moment you tell something to the children, they will say, 'but Dad, what did you do? Don't you think we know what you did in your life? You want us to be perfect, but you are not perfect.'

That is why I said the best thing to do is get right with people, get right with God, confess the mistakes that you made and move on because otherwise you cannot move on. Your life will get stuck. And your family will become dysfunctional. And so now you have no choice but to turn around every time the children do something. Because you do not have the courage to confront them anymore. You are afraid to tell them anything because you are afraid they will shout back at you. So that creates a tremendous problem in a family.

Why do you think we witness cycles of dysfunction right before our eyes? So many families get caught up in this. You do not have to break the curse, you just to face the issue. The grandfather does stuff, foolish stuff and ends up in jail. Spends most of his time in jail, comes out, has a couple more children, goes back to jail and the son sees that and thinks that this is normal. And the son gets caught up in that cycle. And his son ends up in jail and comes back and he has children. And then the third generation grows up thinking that this is normal. My daddy was in jail, my grand-daddy was in jail so this may be normal stuff. The cycles of dysfunction will continue until someone wise up and realize that there is a God out there who can put an end to this. There is a God who loves you, a God who cares about you, a God who cares about your family, a God who cares about your children, a God who cares about your grandchildren. And when we wise up and start calling upon His name and say, 'Lord come and help us, we are helpless, the cycle is continuing and we cannot stop it. Please come and interfere in our family. Please come and do something to stop this cycle. We do not want our children to go through this. We do not want our grandchildren to go through this, we do not want our next generation to go through this.'

God said call unto me and I will answer. He has an answer for you. The system does not have an answer for you. The politicians do not have an answer for you. They issue more and more bonds to build more and more jails, have you noticed that? They are issuing new bonds to create new jails. That is all I think the system can do. But there is a God, who loves you, who cares about you, who cares about your family, who cares about your children, who cares about your grandchildren. He loves you right now, right here!! He can break that bondage right here and put an end to this cycle of dysfunction in your family. But this so called man of God did not realize that. Eventually he came around but it took him awhile. The damage was already done. Dysfunctionality set in and it came to a peak in his conflict with one of his sons called Absalom.

The Bible takes six chapters to tell us this story. If you think God does not care about your family, think again. The Bible took only half a chapter to tell us the story of David's victory over Goliath, the defining moment in his life. But the Bible takes six chapters to tell us the struggle that David had with his son Absalom. So God cares about your family. Your children are important to God. Your family is important to God.

From chapter 13 to 18 we see this ongoing conflict. Since David had multiple wives and he had children with all of them and so all of them are growing up in the same compound. There was one son named Amnon who found another girl Tamar, who was in the same palace but from another wife of David. Both of them are teenagers at that time. The Bible says this young Tamar was extremely beautiful. Amnon was very interested in her but only to have a one night stand.

Sometimes it shudder me to think about the responsibilities of a father. Because whatever you do, your children many repeat it. What did the father do? He found a woman attractive, invited her into his palace through a servant and slept with her. And the son did the same thing. When the father did it, it was with a strange woman from another family. But when the son did it, it was with one of his half sisters.

Amnon used an excuse to get Tamar into his room and raped her. And this young lady was a virgin and she said, 'Listen we know in our culture that cousins are allowed to marry and if you are looking at me as a cousin I can understand. So if you are really interested in me why don't you go and ask our father? Tell our dad that you want to marry me, maybe he will give me as a wife to you.' But he had no interest in getting her as a wife, he just wanted to sleep with her. He pretended to be sick and duped his father into inviting Tamar to his room requesting she make a meal for him. Then he raped her. This extremely beautiful young girl, this princess who wanted to married to a prince, what is she supposed to do with her life now? She is probably thinking, what happened to Bathsheba when my dad did this? A month later she was pregnant. So what if now I am pregnant as a result of this. How am I going to face the world now? It became a big issue for her. So we see her going back to her room, crying through the streets with torn clothes etc.

Absalom was her natural brother and he came across her as she was going back to her room and he said, 'Please don't make a scene. This is family business, so go to your room. Our father will take care of this.' But dad has a big problem, he has no moral authority in that family now. He was afraid to deal with it. The Bible says, when David heard the news he became enraged and shouted at the top of his voice. That is it, nothing happened.

The young man Absalom was watching this and it's his own sister that went through this. So he decided, 'Dad, if you do not do anything about it, one day I will. I am just waiting to see how you will handle this.' Eventually he realized, my dad does not have the guts to handle this. So he found an excuse to get all the princes together and that day he told his cohorts to beat up Amnon and kill him and to make sure he is finished. So Amnon is killed. Bathsheba had a child and God killed that child. Now Amnon is killed by his own brothers and their cohorts. Two children of David are dead now.

When David heard that problems are getting from bad to worse, instead of calling him in and counseling him (which he should have done a long time ago) got angry again. He is afraid to face his own son. He got very angry again and started shouting again, just like many other fathers. When we shout we are sending out a message that we have lost the power. He told his generals to tell Absalom, 'I never want to see his face again.'

Absalom realized he is in big trouble. So this young man ran away to the neighboring country and he stayed there for three years. David never made an effort to reconcile things. So after three years, one of his generals came to a friend and said we have to do something to reconcile things between the father and the son. After all this is the prince! Absalom was an extremely handsome prince and the Bible says there was none more handsome than him in all of Israel. David actually wanted to make him the next King. So this is a person with a tremendous future getting caught up in this cycle of dysfunction. But David is unable to do anything. So the general took the initiative, got a wise woman involved and they played a skit before the King to get the King's attention and finally he said okay. If you guys want him to come back so badly let him come back but I don't want to see his face.

So even though Absalom came back after three years, David did not go and see him. David did not even realize that this is a good opportunity for me to start a new chapter in our relationship. Instead he put him in house arrest. For the next two years he was in house arrest. He never saw David's face. And this young man really loved his dad. When we read the story, we can see that Absalom loved his dad. David had to take the initiative to reconcile the situation. Listen to me dads, our children will mess up, guaranteed. Ask any dads anywhere. We all expect our children to be perfect but they will not be perfect. They will mess up, and when they mess up, shouting at the top of your lungs does not solve anything. Looking the other way does not solve anything. We have to wise up. We have to cease the moment. When God gives us an opportunity to start something fresh; use it wisely. That's the only way you can salvage your family.

I personally know children who have not talked to their dads for 10, 15, 20 years. Both of them are still alive but these children have decided that my dad does not understand me. My dad does not have a clue who I am. He lives in his world and I live in my world. It is a sad thing to see fathers and sons get messed up like that. The role of a father is to train up his your son. He can assume the place of the father when he becomes a mature person. But in so many families it is denied now. And it breaks my heart every time I think about that. I have a good relationship with young people. Many young people tell me this.

David did the same classical mistake. He is right there in the same palace grounds in another building but never used that opportunity to start a fresh chapter in his relationship with his son. So after two years, Absalom said now I am going to do something. And there is a rage building up in up in him because his father is not paying any attention to him. Fathers, do you know that your sons really want your attention? Even when they make the biggest mistake, the best thing you can do . . . in fact, if I go one step further . . . when they make the biggest mistake in their lives, that is the best time to salvage your relationship because they are in a place of willingness to listen to you for a change. All other times they may act like they are wiser than you. But when they really get in trouble instead of jumping all over them if you go and hug them, put your hand around their shoulder and say, 'son I understand we all make mistakes. Dad also has made some mistakes in my life.' That one statement will save your relationship with your son. But unfortunately we are not wise enough to do that. Because we are so ashamed that our children did something stupid, we want to jump all over them. You tell the police you don't have to care of him, I will take care of him. It is natural, but in that process we lose our children though.

Five years went by since the death of Amnon. Everyone should have forgiven that incident and they should have started a new chapter but they did not. And David is not paying any attention to Absalom. So Absalom decided ok, I'm going to act up now. We all know that when children start acting up it is a cry for attention. He said ok, I need some attention! If my dad doesn't want to give me the attention that I deserve then I'm going to get the attention some other way. Do you know what this young man did single handedly? David, the most favorite King in Israel was sitting on the throne alive and well, in perfect health, but his son started a revolt right in front of him and the King did not even realize it. Absalom just showed up one day in front of the palace steps and grabbed a chair and just sat there; everyone knew he was the prince. And the people had forgiven him. The only person who did not forgive him was his father. The people had no problem dealing with Absalom even though they knew what he had done. Isn't that sad?

So here is Absalom, seated by the entrance and when people came with their grievances, he would stop them and say, 'Hey where are you from? Why are you coming to Jerusalem?' And the people would say, 'I have a complaint, I'm going to the King to present my complaint, I need the King to interfere in my business. I need an answer.' And Absalom would say in a nice polished way, 'the King is very busy, you know the King is very busy, he has no time for you.' What he is saying is if the King has no time for me, how is he going to find time for you? So he would say, 'tell me what is your problem and I will give you an answer.' We can see that Absalom was an extremely talented, gifted young person because whatever answer he gave to these people, they accepted it. He knew how to judge things properly even though he got caught in the heat of that emotion in that one moment and killed his half brother. He was a very good and talented person. So one by one all these people started loving Absalom and eventually he single handedly turned the entire nation behind him. And this went on for almost eight years. And the King was not paying any attention! His soldiers would come and say, do you now what your son is doing? Come on man wise up! He is out there taking attention away from you and making you less and less needed in this society. All the people are going after him. Come on, go reconcile with your son at least to save your own throne. But this father would never accept their advice. He totally continued to ignore his son.

Until one day, when the son realized that the whole nation is behind me, he declared an open civil war against his own father. And when we come to chapter 18 we see David running away from his country with a few faithful people. They had heard that Absalom had got a chariot, he has got an army, and his followers were shouting, 'Absalom is the King! Absalom is the King!' Can you imagine the most powerful person in that generation became irrelevant to his subjects! Only because he refused to reconcile with his son!

So now David is running 14 years after Tamar was raped. 14 years wasted, so many opportunities wasted to reconcile. The Bible says, the whole nation (people who were faithful to him) were running after him and everyone of them beating on their chest and crying. David, how can this happen to you? How can this happen in your home? When you are a godly person, when you are a godly King, how can this happen in your home? Because you wasted all the opportunity that God gave you to reconcile!

Fourteen years ago there was a girl, crying through the streets with her clothes ripped and nobody was paying attention. Now an entire nation is crying. This is the price of not handling situations right away. That is why I said none of us will be able to afford the price. You have no choice but to get right with God.

And we all know the end of the story. Absalom was no match to David. David's soldiers were heroes. So Absalom could not stand against David. He was running away on his mule through tamarind trees and his hair got caught up in the branches. The mule ran away here he is hanging between heaven and earth with his hair caught up in a tamarind branch. Somebody came to David's faithful general and said, Absalom is hanging from a tree, this is the best time to finish him off. Despite everything Absalom did, David is still his father. So he asked his soldiers to show Absalom some mercy. But listen fathers, you may feel that way but the society does not feel that way. You may want to show mercy to your children but the society does not care. Society looks at him as a trouble maker. All this trouble is because of this guy and we have a good chance to finish him off and you want us to show mercy? They did not. The general went himself and thrust three spears into his heart and killed this young man with tremendous promise right there.

Look at the end of the story in 2 Samuel 18:33. "Then the King was deeply moved and went up to the chamber over the gate and wept. And as he went he said, thus, oh my son Absalom, my son Absalom, if only I had died in your place. Oh Absalom my son, my son." I know he meant every word of that, every syllable. But if I can speak to David I would say this. David, you did not have to cry like that. Your son did not have to die like that. God gave you fourteen years to reconcile with your son. Only because you refuse to reconcile with your son, you are in this predicament and your son is in this predicament. I want to encourage all of you to use the opportunity God gives you to reconcile with whom you have offended or who may have offended you.

In conclusion, there are six lessons that we can learn from the life of David about fatherhood.

1. Fame and fortune does not dictate a good family. David was the most famous King in Israel but had a messed up family.
2. Involvement is the number one factor. If you want to see your children doing good, get involved. No shortcut for that.
3. Putting off correction is a big mistake. As soon as you see a mistake, whether it is in your life or your children's life, take care of it right away, do not wait for another day.
4. Never allow issues to grow. Deal with them right away. Remember fourteen years was given to David to deal with the issues before God extracted payment from this family.
5. Do not take your children lightly. That was a big mistake that David made. When people came and told him your son is doing campaign against you outside your palace and one day we are all going to get into trouble if you don't deal with this, David did not pay any attention. So many modern day parents make the same mistake. They want to look good for whatever reason and do not correct their children. They take their children lightly.
6. Grudge will always have its own consequences. Take care of the roots of bitterness. The Bible tells us in New Testament, 'do not allow roots of bitterness to grow.' Eventually it will mess up everything. Whether it is in a church or in a family or in your personal life, it will mess up everything.

What is the joy of going into the presence of God without our children? Our family should be number one. Let us make a commitment before God that we will intercede before God until we see all of our children saved. Until we can stand before God one day and boldly proclaim, 'as for me and my household, we shall serve the Lord.' I know all of us do not have that privilege now but don't feel bad. I am not trying to make you feel bad but we must be wise. We must make a decision that if I have to fast I will fast, if I have to spend more time with my children, I will do that, whatever it takes. If I have to beg my children, I will do that. Ask forgiveness for my children, I will do that. Our family comes first. God is interested in our family. Save your family.

CHAPTER XVII

Lessons In Humility

We will be meditating on 2 Samuel 24 and the corresponding passage in 1 Chronicles 21 for this chapter. We will also consider some other passages.

We saw how David was re-established on his throne. Things were going smoothly for a while. The incident we are covering in this chapter happened a while later. Now David is in his sixties and he is an elderly man and when he looks forward, he can see the end of his life. He was more or less very happy with what God had done in his life. He made sure that all the loose ends are taken care of (2 Sam. 21). In other words, as a king he is getting ready to transfer the power to his son. And he can already see Solomon coming up. Initially, if you ask me, David wanted to make Absalom the next king because Absalom was the most handsome and capable among his sons and he had a tremendous personality. He was a tremendous leader. And we know how he single handedly turned the entire nation to his side when a very popular king was still on the throne. But you not only need an amazing personality, you not only need leadership potential but you also need God's favor in your life to get somewhere in life.

Absalom is a classic example of what happens to very talented people who do not depend on God. Even people who grew up through churches and in churches may think they do not need God. They may think, 'Look at me I am a good looking dude. I am very popular and everyone loves me. Wherever I go, I just rise up to the top. I am the cream of the crop. And God has given me all kinds of talents so I do not have to trust in God. I do not have to be very careful with my life. I can just go forward and claim everything for myself and I will be established.' You will be making a big mistake in your life. In fact, when we look around we see so many thousands of capable young people who grew up in the church, came through the ranks in the church, attended Sunday school since the time they were two years old. They know the Bible inside out yet unable to live a productive life. How many thousands of young people are out there in the street today this Sunday morning? Instead of worshiping in a church they are somewhere out in the world, totally lost and confused, not knowing what to do with their life. Only because they thought that they did not need the input of God in their life on a daily basis.

God taught that lesson to Moses almost three thousand five hundred years ago. Moses thought that he could do the same thing. He lived a privileged life. He was educated in the civil and military academies for the princes. He knew he was destined to be the deliverer of Israel. So he thought he could use the knowledge and abilities he had and deliver Israel. One day he killed an Egyptian to help out an Israelite. The next day he ended up running as a refugee from that country. Only then he realized that he could not do this on his own strength. I may have the education, I may have the looks, I may have the money, I may have the influence but I still need God in my life.

God came to Moses and said, 'Moses, don't try to sow among the thorns.' You will only get bruised all over your body. And that is the story of many of our lives including mine. I am somebody who tried this. I tried to go against the will of God and tried to establish my own will in my life only to find out that you only get bruised all over your body when you go against God. So I recommend to you that you surrender your life into the hand of God. Let Him take you where you have to go. Let Him lead you in the right direction and you will be successful in your life.

So David is getting ready to hand the power over to Solomon. If you are following his story in 2 Samuel you can see that in

Chapter 22 and 23, he wrote lengthy Psalms describing his life story and everything that God did for him and how grateful he is to God. So he thought when my time comes I will give the reign over to my son Solomon and go on to eternity. But then came another crisis. Now the crisis had its root in David's mind. Why would David go through another crisis on top of everything that he already went through in his life? That is because the enemy does not give up. Remember we spoke about that. He is a roaring lion just looking for ways to come and devour you. And he wants to mess up what God is doing. He has one plan, from generation to generation and it is this—he wants to mess up what God is trying to do. If he sees that God is using you, he is going to do his best to mess up your life. If God is trying to do something through a church he will try to infiltrate that church and he will try to mess up that church. If you are having a beautiful family life and people are saying look at you and saying 'what a marvelous couple, what a model couple,' let me tell you Satan is listening to that. And Satan will try to infiltrate into your family life and mess up your family life because he cannot stand God's name being glorified through your family life.

So while David is getting ready to hand everything over to Solomon, he is making a count of everything he has. Remember one of the desires of his heart was to build a beautiful temple for God. So he had amassed a lot of silver and gold and he started counting. He was taking the amount of gold he has accumulated. He was taking the amount of silver that he had accumulated. He was taking the amount of cedar wood that he had accumulated. And while he was doing all of this which was okay, Satan planted a thought in his mind. None of us are beyond the schemes of Satan. The moment you think you are beyond that, that guarantees your downfall. What David was doing was natural. He was just making a note, did I accumulate enough gold for that temple my son is promised to build for my God? And do I have enough silver here, do I get enough cedar wood here? It was all a natural process but in the midst of that natural process, Satan entered into his mind and planted a little seed there.

David is looking at Solomon and realized that this boy is not like me. This boy is not a man of war. I could defeat Goliath, I could defeat the Philistines time after time. I could go after any nation that came against us. We had victories after victories. I inherited a little nation and it has become huge because God used me to expand the boundaries of this nation. I was a man of war and I would not have to worry about what the enemies would do. Then he looked at Solomon and he realized that Solomon is a man of peace. The Bible itself calls him a man of peace. That is because he had no interest in war. David had a set up a beautiful military academy and the first person to flunk from that military academy was his son Solomon. He had no interest in war. He did not want to do anything with war. He never went and visited with the generals. He would never hang out with the soldiers. He never took a sword in his hands. He never took a shield in his hand and David is watching all of this and there is a little bit of fatherly concern in his mind. He is wondering, yes this country is established now, yes we have a huge nation now, and we are a very wealthy nation now but what is going to happen once somebody comes against this nation? It is that fatherly concern that got him in trouble now.

One of the lessons that God has taught me is this: Even though we are children of God, even though we have faith, we believe in God, sometimes we begin to start thinking negative thoughts about our children. It is because of our concern and because we love them but we should not. You know why? Satan can use that negative thought as a seed to bring destruction later on in their life. Before you start to look at yourself as a father and before you look at yourself as a mother you should first look at yourself as a child of God. You should have the confidence that God is going to come through and establish His will in my children's life. So all I have to do is commit my children into his hands. It does not matter where they are today, it does not matter how good or bad they are today. It does not matter even if they are totally going against the will of God in their life. As a child of God there is only one thing that I need to do. All I need to do is bring my child to the altar and pray over him and allow God to move and establish His plans for my children. And God will do it.

David got carried away and wanted to make sure even if Solomon is not interested in the war, if somebody comes against him while he is on the throne, they had enough soldiers in the army. Satan got him worried and planted that thought in David's mind. It was because Satan wanted to rise up against the continuous progress that was happening in that nation. So David called his generals to do a census of the soldiers. How do we know this? When we read this chapter, they only counted the soldiers! Even though David said he is going to take a census of the whole nation, he did not. He only counted the soldiers. And this is when I realized what was going through David's mind. He wanted to make sure that there were enough soldiers in the land to protect my son and his throne. So they started counting and his generals had better judgment in this matter than the king.

They went to the king and said, don't do this. It is not because of our power that we had victory. Remember when you had victory over Goliath as a young man? You had nobody to support you. You were all alone at battle and you single handedly defeated that enemy. It was not because you are a seasoned soldier. You were nothing but a little boy. So how did you have that tremendous victory? Because God was in your life! So what we really need for victory is the presence of God in our life not the soldiers. It does not matter how many soldiers we have, we really need God. So let us continue to put our trust in God. But David because he was so worried about Solomon, insisted on knowing how many soldiers they had. The Bible tells us that he overruled them and ultimately what the king wants gets done will be done. They took the number and they found out that there were this amount of soldiers in Judah and this many soldiers in Israel. Judah was the first tribe that God said should lead into the battle. And then all the other 11 tribes together they found out how many soldiers they had. So David was happy for a moment. And then he realized that he fell into a trap. Look at 1 Chron. 21:1, "Now Satan stood up against Israel and moved David to number Israel". David did not get it initially. He didn't know what Satan was using his fatherly concerns to get in and bring destruction. You have to be very careful. You should not submit to every thought that passes through your mind. As children of God we must sit in the presence of God and make sure that these thoughts are really coming from God. Only after that you should surrender to those thoughts. Sometimes the thoughts may look very innocent. You may think, what is the big deal of taking a census? Every nation takes census. But this was not a regular census. He didn't even take the whole census, he only counted the soldiers. So he was just trying to make sure everything is in place before he left the scene. Only after that process was done, while they were coming back to him with the numbers did he wake up. He is a child of God after all and he woke up and he realized that he made a mistake. I allowed Satan to use me. And why was God so upset about this whole process anyway?

Remember we looked at three things that God had told the leaders in Israel. We looked at that passage in Deuteronomy 16 and one of the things was that they should never be self-reliant. And God said this in a different way. He said, 'don't increase the chariots and horses for you.' In other words, don't increase the size of your army so much that you don't trust in Me anymore. Make sure that there never will be a day you look at your army and say now even if God is not with us we can have victory because we have such a huge army. And what is David trying to do? He is trying to make sure they were self-reliant.

Immediately he became guilty and he realized he had done something wrong. And he called the prophet, the seer who was giving him advice or his spiritual advisor and said I did something wrong. Now what do I do? We also have to understand this in our life. We have to be very careful about pride entering into our life. All of us are prone to pride. Nobody is exempt from it including me because I can say a good message one Sunday and at the end of the service ten people come to me and say, 'Pastor, that was an awesome message' and by the time the tenth person comes, I go up two inches. It is only natural, we are human beings. Pride can enter into us in every area and one thing that God hates is pride. The Bible teaches us that pride comes before the fall. Solomon told us that in the book of Proverbs. The day you feel proud of yourself, you are setting yourself up for a big fall. Greater your height when pride enters into your life, the greater will be your fall.

We know that is what happened with Lucifer. He was the first worship leader in the universe. The Bible says he was created in such a way that all he had to was just open his wings and beautiful music would come. All he had to do was just fly around and spread his wings and every time he spread his wings, every note in the octave came through. And God's throne will be filled with music. And they had a huge choir in heaven, if you allow me to put my own two cents in here. The Bible tells us that when Lucifer fell, 1/3 of the angels fell with him. So if you ask me my interpretation about that is that the choir in heaven is so huge that it comprised 1/3 of all the angels of God. And this is a worship leader with a huge choir and singing beautifully in the throne room of God and filling heaven with melodious music. But then, one day, pride entered into his heart. And he looked at himself and he said look at all these angels mesmerized by my worship and talent. He forgot that he was a created being for a moment. He forgot that he had all of that because somebody gave it to him. He looked at God and said even He is impressed with my worship. Everyone in this universe is impressed with my worship. Oh what a great person I am. And because he was created as an angel he could not be killed. Angels are created without death. They can be put to eternal punishment but they cannot be killed even by God because God does not violate His own law.

Lucifer looked at God and said, I am next to Him. If I can put my throne above His throne then this entire thing will be under my control and I will run this universe in a completely different way. And he started telling all of the choir members, I am not happy with the way God is running this universe. I have some new ideas in my mind. God in an ancient being and He is thinking way too old fashioned and you know he has been around forever. We need some fresh blood in here. We need some fresh thought in here. He is ancient of days. If I am given the reign of this universe, I have some fresh ideas in mind, only if God will give me a chance but I know He will never give up His throne. So we have to do something. We have to usurp a rebellion and push Him off His throne. And then this universe would be much better. Look what pride does to you.

When pride enters into you, you really forget who you are. He forgot that he is a created being. He forgot that he has talents because someone gave it to him. And he forgot that this person who gave him that talent can take that away from him. And one moment you are an angel of light because God created you with goodness and positivity in your life and wanted to make you a blessing for this whole universe so while you are moving at that level, you are an angel of light. God did create him as an angel of light. But the moment God took all these away from him, his personality changed. He became nothing but darkness. You and I are good today because God is in our life. We are positive beings because God is in our life today. Because when God is in your life and you look into the world and you read about the serial killers and rapists and all these people and you begin to wonder how can somebody sink that low? How is it possible that another human being just like me sink to that low and turn like that? When God's presence is taken away from your life there is nothing but darkness in your life and no one can measure the depth of that darkness. You can sink below the level of beasts, you can sink below the level of the animals in the field and you begin to wonder and look at that person and say what happened to this person?

Pride is damaging. The moment that God feels your focus is shifting from God, God will deal with that. And that is what happened in the life of Abraham even though it is not explicitly mentioned in that fashion in the Bible. God looked at how Abraham was always playing with Isaac and spending way too much time with Isaac the son, he got in his elderly age. God just wanted to make sure his heart was for Him. So one day he came into Abraham's life in Genesis 22:3, and God said, 'take your son, your only begotten son and take him to a place that I will show you and offer him as a burn offering.' And we know that God is not into human sacrifice. God detests that practice and wiped away the nations that used to practice that in ancient history. So how come the God came into the life of Abraham and asked him to take his only son to a mountain top and offer him as a burn sacrifice? The sacrifice was never going to happen. God just wanted to know where Abraham's heart was. And that is why sometimes God moves in your life in special ways. Sometimes God will move in inexplicable ways and God will make demands that he will never make on anyone else. And you begin to wonder what is wrong with God. How come is making this so difficult for me? I don't see God doing the same thing with other people. Does he have anything against me? No, he just wants to know where you heart is. He just wants to make sure you still love him the way you used to love him. He's not against the blessings in your life. He has nothing against your children, nothing against your car, nothing against your house, nothing against your bank balance. He has nothing against the blessings in your life. He just wants to make sure you still love him the same way you used to love him when you had an empty bank account and you had nothing in your life. God wants to make sure that he is still number one in our lives. That's why Jesus told his disciples in Luke 14:33, that "whoever of you does not forsake all that he has cannot be my disciple." Then he told them to forsake their parents, forsake their siblings, their family etcetera. Jesus was not saying that you should not get married if you are a disciple of Jesus. In church history a lot of people made that mistake. From second century, a lot of people did not get married when they became priests or bishops and eventually it became part of the practice of Christendom. That is not what Jesus meant. Jesus did not say you cannot get married or you cannot have a family or to walk out on your parents. What he meant was, make sure that I am number one. Make sure I am number one, not your parents. Make sure I am number one, not your children. Make sure I am number one, not the blessings that I have to you.

David never expected Satan to enter so late in his life when he is just getting ready to hand everything over to his son. That is why we have to be vigilant. 2 Corinthians 10:2 tells us that we must ready to pull down every stronghold that rises up against the excellence of the knowledge of Jesus Christ. That stronghold will keep coming into your life. Satan will bring it up again. When you pull down one, another one comes up. When you pull down that one another one comes up. So you have to be vigilant. You have to be always on the lookout and keep ourselves humble.

There is a favorite verse of mine in the book of Habakkuk because I had to pray that prayer many times in my life. In Habakkuk 3:2, "Oh Lord, revive your work in the midst of the years. In the midst of the years make it known in wrath remember mercy." That last phrase is so much a part of my thinking, "in wrath remember mercy." That is who God is. If you read that book, you see that God was talking about coming judgment and then God told the prophet write it down in big letters on a board and plant it by the roadside so even when the people were running by, they could see it. It is so big that everyone will read it. What was the message that they were reading? That judgment is coming. Then God gave him a hint and said it is not coming now. God said, 'wait for it, it will come.' Then Habakkuk woke up from that vision and realized the judgment is coming but it is not coming right away. So he decided to make use of that time. He started interceding for his nation in the presence of God. And this is part of that prayer that Habakkuk prayed and he said, "Oh Lord, revive your work in the midst of the years." Before the years run out and judgment actually show up, Lord. Revive it so the judgment does not have to come.

And he said, Lord I know you are angry but in the midst of your anger do not forget to show mercy because you are also a merciful God. Isn't that the story of our life folks? Even when He gets angry, the Bible tells us that He cannot forget His nature. What is His nature? He is the father of compassion. He is a compassionate God. Even this morning he's a compassionate God. It doesn't matter what you did with your life last week, it doesn't matter how you made God angry last week. In the midst of that he will still show mercy. He cannot change his nature folks. He's a merciful God. So if you need mercy in your life, all you have to do is just reach out to Him. Just call upon his name He will come through for you. He will extend his mercy into your life.

So once David found out that he made a mistake as a child of God he decided to get back into the presence of God. He is looking for ways to get back into the presence of God. He called the prophet and he confessed. Now I want to give you some principles going on from here. Principal number one, restoration is not possible before confession. Everyone wants restoration in their life. But people are too proud to humble themselves before God and say, 'Lord, I messed up.' The moment you acknowledge, you open the door for the compassion of the God to come into your life. And then God will take over and He will show you ways to get back into His presence. And that is what God did with David.

The second thing is, when he did that God sent somebody to him. God sent a prophet to him and God gave him an option. I don't know since when God gives us an option before he decides to punish us. It is not the usual way of God deal with us. God doesn't come to us and say, 'I am going to send you into unemployment for one year. I am going to let your car be repossessed or I am going to let your house go into foreclosure. Choose which one you want. God does not do that usually but God did that for David. Why, because he was a man after God's own heart. He was a true worshipper.

Even though Satan entered into his mind and caused him to create another crisis in their land, he woke up immediately. He realized his mistake before God sent somebody to remind him. That was not the story before. In this case even before God sent somebody to remind he woke up and he realized he messed up. I have violated what you asked of me as a leader in Israel so what should I do now. So God said, 'I can appreciate that, I can see your heart. I'm going to give you three options. I'm going to send you a plague in your land or a famine in your land which will last much longer or I'm going to let the enemies come and defeat you. Select what you want.' David only had one answer. He didn't pick one but he avoided one. The answer that he gave to God was this: 'Let me not fall into the hand of men.' That means, 'I am too old to run God. I have been running all my life. When I was young, people were chasing me all over but now I am too old to run. So please don't let enemies come and defeat us and make me run from this nation.' The other two he said he doesn't mind. And David put the ball back into God's court.

Let's turn to 2 Sam. 24:15, this is what God did, "So the Lord sent a plague in Israel from the morning until the appointed time. From Dan to Bathsheba, seventy thousand men and people died." I was trying my best to figure out what was that plague that caused the death of seventy-thousand people but no one knows. The bible does not allow us to figure that out. It could have been a torrential rain because in the Middle East they are not used to torrential rains. Because of that, whenever rain came, we know from the Bible, it usually came with hail, huge ball sized hail. It could have been hail but we don't know exactly what it was. Whatever it was seventy-thousand people fell in three days. Even though it said for its appointed time, God said I will send the plague for three days. Not because they did anything wrong but because their leader went wrong.

These people were innocent. A leader never falls alone. When a leader falls he will always take a whole bunch of people with him. So this is how it ends, the plague came. God may have forgiven our sins but we still have to suffer the consequences of what we did. That's built into that sowing and reaping principle that God established in the universe. So you cannot escape from it. God forgave David but still the nation had to suffer because of what he did.

As soon as David surrendered, we can see that God began to move. There is something unusual about the picture in 1 Chronicles 21 that helps us learn how God functions. If you know how God functions, then you will know how to handle situations. We know judgments can come but this is one of the passages in the Bible that teaches us that when God sends judgment, God entrusts that judgment with an angel. David being a spiritual person is trying to get back into the presence of God and he is seeing these innocent people being killed because of the sin in his life and he is wondering and looking for a loophole to get back into the presence of God. He knew there must be something he could do.

So he started looking in the spiritual realm. What is happening here? How is God carrying out the judgment? There must be a way out because the Bible teaches us that with every trial there is also a way out. All of a sudden he saw an angel standing with a pulled up sword in his hand and he realized that this is the person is in charge of this judgment. And as long as that sword is lifted up the judgment would continue. He realized that there is only one way to stop this judgment, somehow I have to get his sword back in its sheath. In 1 Chronicles 21, the Bible tells us that as soon as David saw that he called all the generals and all the minister and said come on lets fall down before God. Let us surrender ourselves and let us ask for His mercy because somehow we have to find a way a stop this.

Sometimes we go through situations and you may be in the midst of a judgment. You can look around in your life, in your business, in your financial affairs or in your family and see a sword lifted up and you see the judgment coming. Somehow you have to get that sword down. Otherwise there is no way out for you. There is no way the judgment can be over until the sword comes down. And there is no way the sword is going to come down unless you fall prostrate before the Lord and surrender yourself. How many families do I know who is going through issues after issues? For generations going through issues after issues, but they are too proud to humble themselves before God. Humble yourself, give room for His compassion to come through in your life so that judgment can be stopped. But people are so proud! They rather suffer judgment than yield themselves to God. He will show compassion if you surrender yourself. That is why the Bible says now is the accepted time.

Don't you want the judgment to stop in your home? Don't you want it to come to an end? Aren't you tired of the judgment? Then how come we do not surrender ourselves into the hand of God. How come we do not humble ourselves? Let us develop the understanding Habakkuk had and pray 'before the years are over, show mercy.'

The moment that David and the ministers and all of them surrendered before God, God sent a decree to that angel to stop his hand. It did not take any time. The moment they surrendered God sent out that decree. And David is watching all of this and he saw that the angel was facing the nation and the judgment was happening all over the nation. But in the nick of time he surrendered before God. And when he surrendered before God and looked up, he saw that the angel of God had turned around toward Jerusalem. It was going to hit home. Jerusalem was next. But the spirit of God moved in his heart at the right time to surrender. And before the judgment was initiated in the city of Jerusalem, which was going to be the city of God, it was stopped.

Do you know why you are delivered? Somebody saw God's sword turning towards you and had the spiritual wisdom to fall on their knees and start interceding on your behalf. God, wake up somebody! Some mother, some grandmother somewhere in the middle of the night, shake them up in the midst of their sound sleep and cause them to get up!! Let them start praying for this grandson, this granddaughter because a sword is coming and it is about to fall on their life!!! And you think because you are smart, because you are slick, you escaped judgment. No, it is because God caused somebody to fall on their knees on your behalf. Somebody was crying, somebody was shedding tears, somebody was fasting, and somebody was calling upon God that's why you are here. That is why I am here ministering to you.

When David saw that angel with the pulled out sword, the Bible tells us he was standing at a threshing field of a man named Arounna. We must pay attention to that statement. Where was David standing? On a mount in the city of Jerusalem. And we already saw that the city of Jerusalem was on top of a mountain that was about two thousand feet high. And he is looking from there and next to him on the other side is the boundary there is a threshing field! And he sees this angel standing there with the sword. Have you ever wondered why would there be a threshing field two thousand feet high in the air? Have you ever seen a threshing field two thousand feet in the air? So we know that that is not a regular threshing field. Then what was that?

It was a field prepared to worship the gentile deities, the fertility Gods. Because down in the valley were their fields and the regular threshing fields. And they wanted to make sure that their harvest would come in safely. So they prepared a place of worship two thousand feet high on top of a mountain in the form of a threshing field. And this man Ornan was the high priest of that worship system. He was the owner of that property and the high priest of that worship system. So his job was to go over to the threshing field and pay homage to the deities.

When the angel came down, even though God sent the angel, that threshing field became his foothold. Understand this spiritual principle. When you leave room for Satan in your home, that becomes the foothold for the angel of judgment. So the only way you can make sure that these kinds of things will not happen in your life is to make sure you get rid of that threshing field.

Get rid of that space, get rid of the room where you may be keeping images of saints or whatever. Today it has become fashionable to purchase idols as curio objects and keep them in your living room etc. People in the west do not know that these are not made on an assembly line to be sold in the market as souvenirs. These are idols made by families whose only family business is to make images of their gods. They get up early, bathe themselves, sanctify themselves before they make the images of their gods. Then they pray over them and take them to the market to sell them. The western tourists think they are just cute looking souvenirs and buy them and bring them to their living rooms. Then all of a sudden things start happening in your life and in your home. And you being to wonder, how come these things never used to happen in my house before but now they are? These things can bring curses upon your home, curses upon your children, curses upon your family, bind your finances and put you through all kinds of unwanted issues. That is why God warned old testament Israelites not to be enticed by the images of their neighboring cultures and not to bring any of those images home. Do yourself a favor. Dump them, get rid of them because when you have God you do not need anything else. Do not allow a parallel altar to God in your home. God is very particular about that. (Remember what God demanded from Gideon?) Not only that, when the judgment comes it becomes the foothold for it. And David saw the angel in charge of that judgment standing in the threshing field of Ornan.

Even David did not know what to do at that time and the prophet came into his life. This is the third principle I want to share with you from this story. When you are going through crisis you need somebody to give you advice. You need spiritual advice in your life. It can be your pastor. It can be your prayer partner. It can be a seasoned man or woman of God. You need somebody to give you an idea or a good word. David saw angels standing there and David realized there was something unusual about that. The angel is standing in that threshing field but he did not know what to do. So here come Gad into his life again and he said God showed you that to show you a way to come out of the judgment. So run to that place. Buy that place and clean up that place and erect an altar for God so that judgment will never come again against Jerusalem.

In your life and my life also, we must understand this principle. If we do not want the judgment to come back you have to cleanse the place. You have to cleanse that foothold that Satan used to bring the judgment. And Gad advised David to pay the price and purchase that place so nobody would make a claim on it. Make sure the deed is in your name. Which means that no one can come and make a claim on that property any more. It is a picture of total deliverance. Satan cannot come back and make a claim on that property anymore. We have to wise up folks. If Satan is using something in your family make sure that area is cleaned up. So that Satan can never come back and make claim on it. Sometimes you have to purchase that back.

I look at life differently now than I used to ten years ago. Because the more you get to know the Bible, the more you study the Bible, you have a more spiritual outlook towards things. So do not be shocked at what I am about to share. Sometimes Satan can use one of your children to create havoc in your home. You are a child of God and you truly serve God but Satan does not care. Satan will tell you, if I cannot get into you I will come around and find a loop hole and get into your house through someone else in your family. And when Satan does that, you know what you have to do based on this principle is purchase it back. Gad told David, go to Ornan's threshing field and make sure Satan will never make a claim on that again and so purchase it. Pay the price for it and make it your own. If Satan is using one of your children to create havoc in your home to remove the peace from your home, purchase that child back. And do you know what the purchase price that you have to pay to get that child back? It's the blood of the Lamb of God!!!! Plead the blood of Jesus over your child as you intercede for him or her. You have deliverance available because of His shed blood on the cross. If you are tired of Satan playing games with you, playing games with your children, taking the peace from your home, binding up your finances, attacking your health again and again then this is the moment, this is the day to get deliverance. Let the sword is pulled back from your life and from your family.

CHAPTER XVIII

The Heart of a Godly Leader

Let us look at the life of David as a leader. We are a generation that is very interested in leadership. Many of you are in leadership positions and you have plans and goals for your life. And you want to see advancement in your life. And there are always things to learn from other people whom God raised up to be leaders in history and you can always learn from them and that is what we will do here.

Let us turn to Psalm 78, verses 70 to 72 and look at the testimony about the leadership of David given by another man a few generations later. "He also chose David his servant, and took him from the sheepfolds; from following the ewes that had young and brought him to shepherd Jacob his people, and Israel his inheritance. So he shepherded them according to the integrity of his heart; and guided them by the skillfulness of his hands."

We have already seen that God had promised the Israelites that someday they will have a king. In the early formative days of that society, God wanted to be their king. It was a theocratic society. God was ruling them directly through prophets and judges whom he raised up for each generation but God said that is not forever. Eventually you will have a king. And then God set up the standard for that king. In Deuteronomy 17:15-17, God set up the standards for the kings that will be coming and ruling Israel later. God told them that they must be different from other leaders. And that is basically the focus of our study in this chapter. Christianity needs leaders, Christianity has leaders and Christianity cannot continue without leadership. But Christian leaders are supposed to be different than other leaders. And how we are supposed to be different from other leaders will be the focus of our study.

In the book of Deuteronomy, chapter 16, God had expressly prohibited them from accumulating three different things. First of all, God said they could not use the leadership position to make money for themselves. They should not amass wealth for themselves. Secondly, God said they should not build a huge army. I want them to trust in me when they go into battle, rather than their chariots and their horses. And then it was very common in those days for people in leadership positions to be engaged in polygamy and have multiple wives. And God said, in Israel it should not be like that. You should only have one wife but we know that many of the Israel leaders did not keep that particular command from God. So God told them this about thirty-five hundred years ago. You can have leadership, you need leadership but your leadership should be different. They should set an example for the rest of the world. They must be a light for others so that others know what is in the heart of God. Even today that is exactly what God expects from us.

Leadership is not only important it is crucial. Henry Blackaby, one of the highly respected Christian leaders, says in his book "Spiritual Leadership" that "the greatness of an organization will be directly proportional to the greatness of its leaders". No organization can grow beyond the limits of a leader.

In our studies we also focused on the life of king Saul who was on the throne before David came on the scene. We saw that one of the reasons that the nation struggled when he was on the throne was because of the limitations of his personality.

If you really want to be a leader, whether you want to be a Pastor or a businessman, or a bank manager or an IT manager or a Supervisor or you plan to set up an organization with franchises all over, whatever is your dream, you have the freedom to dream that as a Christian. There are certain kinds of businesses that I believe children of God should not enter into. But almost any kind of business you can get into as long as you obey the principles God has put in place.

If God has called you into ministry, make sure you spend time in the presence of God and clarify your call. Ask God questions, say 'Lord I have this feeling you have called me for something and there is a desire in my heart to do something for you. I know you placed that desire there because that is not a human desire. What do you want me to do with this desire? Why did you put this desire in my heart?' Human beings just want to take care of themselves. So if you feel like you want to do something for God, it is a God given desire, it is not a natural desire. So you start asking questions to God. Once God make things clear to you then you can go in that direction. You begin to see God's grace upon you. One way you figure out why God has called you is to see where the grace of God begins to come through. If you want to go forward in the area where God has called you, you have to develop leadership skills. With your natural gifting you can only go so far. We will see that David had a very lengthy training period.

Let me start with why Saul failed as a leader. We know that people selected Saul. They had a couple of criteria. They wanted their king to be good looking. When we present our king before the rest of the nations he must be impressive. That was their first criteria, they did not start with God. People went for looks. Then he assumed the throne and the reality began to hit and they began to see what kind of man he was.

We see that first of all there was a weakness in his decision making skills. He was very arbitrary and unreasonable in his demands as a king or in his decisions made as a king. This is evident in 1 Kings, chapter 14. The nation of Israel was at a war. When you go to war, you have to take sword and spear to fight and you need energy. But this king decided that day to declare as a national fast. And he said if anyone eats anything today I am going to kill that person. What happened is that his own son did not know about that. So after a few hours he got tired and he was looking for something to eat and found a honeycomb and ate it. Then the father found out. Jonathan his son has become a hero in front of the rest of the people but his father got very angry with him and said, 'I made a decree today that nobody should eat and you ate a honeycomb so surely you must die.' This is immediately after he heard that he won the battle for that nation. The people had to rise up and say, 'You are not going to kill this young man because he is the one who won the victory for us today.' So he was very poor in decision making.

The second thing was that he did not know the limits as a king. In 1 Samuel 18, we see that he was a king but he also wanted to become the priest. In order for an organization to function well, there must be checks and balances. Every leader has limits. Kings in Israel had limits. Kings were not supposed to be priests. In 1 Samuel 18 we see an incident where Samuel was late and Saul all of a sudden told the people to bring the sacrifice, I will do the sacrifice myself. And we know that God got extremely angry because he was assuming a post that was not given to him. God told him, 'I am taking the kingdom away from you as a result of this disobedience.' He did not know his limits.

And the third thing was that he was only worried about himself and his family. Unfortunately, there are Pastors who do that too. It happens in many churches in this country. It is like a home business for the Pastor. It is for his sake, and it is for his wellbeing and his children's wellbeing etcetera. When you begin to think like that God slowly begins to pull back. You cannot mix your ideas with God's ideas. Either you go with your ideas or you go with God. And when you try to mix the two of them together that's when God slowly pulls back and God's presence leave those places.

That is what happened with King Saul. He was worried about Jonathan. When God started using David and started bringing David up, he was always worried about Jonathan. He would start cussing Jonathan and would jump on him saying in effect, 'You are a foolish person. Can't you see that David is coming up and can't you see that when he comes up your position will be in jeopardy? How come you are not protecting your position?' Jonathan was a real godly man and he said, 'Hey, if God wants to use him its fine with me. Let him sit on the throne, let me be the second in the kingdom, I do not want to fight with him.' But the father could not take that and he became very jealous and he became enraged. Remember all those years he chased David trying to kill him to save the throne for Jonathan? But in the end he ended up killing himself and killing his son in that process. He was too worried about his family to go with God.

His fourth leadership weakness was *lording over the people*. Look at this passage in Mark 10:42. "But Jesus called them to himself and said to them, you know that those who are considered rulers over the Gentiles lorded over them; and their great ones exercise authority over them. Yet it shall not be so among you; but whoever desires to become great among you, shall be your servant. And whoever of you desires to be first; shall be slave of all." And then he added and said, "For even the son of man did not come to be served but to serve and to give his life as a ransom for many." Jesus is saying that, Christian leadership is different; spiritual leadership is different. You are not lording over the people.

Recently I and my wife were watching on CNN a presentation about Rev. Jim Jones. We were shocked by what we saw. How can a thousand people submit themselves to the whims of a crazy demoniac? He was initially a Pastor but later on from his lifestyle that he was demon possessed. And yet these people were so used to this man issuing decrees for so many years, subjugated to that so that they could not break loose. When you see that final picture of 900+ people killed by injecting cyanide into their body and people submitting themselves for that, you wonder how is that possible? It is possible because people get used to things after a while. And that is why God set up a standard for spiritual leadership. Jesus said, 'Gentiles can do that, Idi Amin can do that but a Christian leader is different. A Christian leader is not supposed to be Joseph Stalin? A Christian leader is not supposed to be Mao or Sadaam Hussein. So lording over people is not allowed in Christiandom.

His fifth leadership weakness was partial obedience to God. In 1 Samuel 13, we see that there was no room for guidance from God in Saul's life. When God would tell him to do things one way he would go another way. So God's directions ceased in his life. It came to a point where he desperate for guidance from somewhere. And we know that towards the end of his life he started seeking out witches to get guidance from them because God stopped talking to him. And that is why it was a failed leadership. And so that's not an example for us to follow.

Then what is the kind of leadership that God want his people to have? We get a glimpse of it in Psalm 78:70-72. In those three verses we can see elements of a type of leader that God wants over his people and it is known as the shepherd king. It is shepherding not lording. And that is what God told about David. In verse 70, "He also chose David his servant and took him from the sheep folds and following the ewes that had young. He brought him to shepherd Jacob his people". So shepherding is the model.

Shepherding is the model of Christian leadership. And you know the word Pastor actually comes from shepherding, both in Greek and in Hebrew. A Pastor is a shepherd. That is why in Christian churches we refer to our Pastors as our shepherds, not the Lords. I don't reign over you, I am called to model a style of leadership for you so that you can follow it. Look in verse 70 again. God said this about David, 'I gave him training.' It also says, "He called him from the sheep folds following the ewes that had young.' That means God started training David when he was a little boy.

Your life experiences are very valuable. Many times we look at our life experiences and think it just happens. No it is not. It happens for a purpose. God is putting you through a school. Everything you go through in your life is a training ground for what is ahead of you. And you can make good use of everything that happens in your life. Both negative and positive. You can you use it for God's glory later in your life.

When David was young, his father forsook him, his mother forsook him and even though he had seven older brothers they did not go after the sheep. The little boy David was sent out with the sheep. We saw that it looked like an unjustifiable act in the natural but God said don't worry I was training you. When people are unjust to you, God looks at that situation and says don't worry I let it happen in your life. When people forsook you God said, don't worry they forgot about you because I allowed that to happen so that I can give you some specific training. Even when your boss bypasses you on that promotion which you were counting on, God said, don't worry I knew it. But I allowed it as specific training so that I can use you in the future. All those years when David was chasing the sheep, it looked like it was a waste of time.

One specific thing that God mentioned was the ewes were the little ones. That means the milking sheep and baby sheep. God said, 'I allowed you to walk behind them for a reason. I don't know how many of you had goats or sheep in your home. I always had sheep in my home when I was growing up. So I know when a sheep has a baby sheep it does not walk very fast. It takes one step turns around and looks for its baby and takes another step and looks behind for its baby. And poor David is waiting for the sheep to catch up because all the good and young ones have run way up in the front and waiting for these mother sheep to come along.

Can you see any relevance to this in a Christian organization? We have people who are healthy, people for whom everything is going okay in their life and they just want to run. Because they have good jobs, they have good cars, they have good houses, their marriage is okay, they have plenty of money in the bank, nothing is wrong with any area of their lives so they are in a rush. They say, come on Pastor let's move! Let's run! But a Pastor cannot do that because there are others who are going through issues after issues in the same church. A pastor has to stay with them and probably the other people will get upset. Pastor, you are too slow and taking too long, come on catch up with us. But a Pastor cannot because God put him as Pastor over the entire congregation. Not only over the people who are doing good. Not just over the people who are doing bad but for the whole congregation. So he has to have a heart for the whole congregation.

And God said, David, remember the days when you had to stand and wait for the mother sheep to catch up? I was training you because one day you are going to be the king and I did not want you to forget the people who are suffering in your kingdom. I don't want you to just focus on the people for whom everything is just okay; people who have money; people who have prestige; and people who have position and all these things. I wanted you to have a heart to take care of the humble folks in your kingdom.

And I put you through that training so that it will come natural to you. Remember the first thing that he did after he became king? He called his servants and said, 'if there is someone in the household of Saul that I may show mercy on behalf of my friend Jonathan?' He went and found this paralyzed young man called Mephibosheth and people had to carry him into the kings presence. And usually you don't get to sit at the kings table if you are a paralyzed person. Everything must be okay with you. You must be able to stand up and salute the king when the king enters. This was a paralyzed man but David took him and gave him a seat at his table and said, you can have food with me for every meal. Why? Because of the training God gave him and also because God expected his kings to be shepherds. In the Old Testament they were supposed to be shepherd kings and in the New Testament leadership also we are supposed to be shepherds. And that is why David wrote Psalm 23 addressing God as a shepherd.

2 Samuel, chapter 7 is another passage that came to my attention. That is when God came down and gave a lot of promises to the house of David and told him that every generation there will be somebody to sit on the throne. I will not remove my grace from your family as I have removed from the household of Saul. In response to that, when David started praying in verses 18-21, you can see how many times David repeated the phrase, 'oh sovereign Lord.' He was saying that you are the real sovereign. A king is considered the sovereign. But he is saying that you are the real sovereign. I just do your work. I have been given a throne but I am just doing your work. That is the attitude of a real child of God. Putting God first in everything and giving God the honor. So the first thing that God expects from a spiritual leader is an attitude to be a shepherd and not to lord over people.

The second thing we see in Sam 78 is the integrity of heart. That means that you must enter into this business with pure motives and best intentions. Your motives must be pure. If you want God's blessing upon your ministry you must be pure. You are wasting your time if you think that you can deceive God. And we know that so many people have entered into ministry with impure motives. We know that many people get into ministry to make money. I mean some of these people on TV you just follow along with them and you can see that they are only interested in money and that is the only thing that comes out of their mouth.

Integrity of the heart means highest ethical and moral standards. But at the same time we also know that David was not a perfect man. A number of times he made mistakes. Not only in the case of Bathsheba. We saw that he counted people against God's will. He went against God's will at least three different times. So how can God talk about him as a man who has integrity of heart? This is what it means, I think. Sometimes you set a high standard for yourself and you fall short of that high standard. And when that happens to you, God can see that and he understands that. God looks at you with compassion. But then there are people who set up very low standards, who have impure motives, selfish motives and do things in a callus way. And God knows the difference between the two. That is why when man looks at our outside, God looks at our hearts. We know the cry of David. Every time something would happen, he would go into the presence of God and say, 'Lord I didn't mean to do that. I never thought this would happen in my life. I don't know how it can happen when I am a child of God. I am a worshipper but Lord I messed up in this area. I know I did something against your will.' And God always gave him grace because God could see his heart. That he was truly repentant and that he was sorry for what he did.

The third thing that is mentioned in this passage is that he *led the people with skillful hands.* That is because of the training period. That means you have to work hard. If God has given you a leadership position you have to work hard. A leader cannot afford to stop growing. For example, a Pastor must have something fresh to give to the people every Sunday. You must be able to say what I have been able to receive from the Lord, I have given to you. That was the testimony of Apostle Paul. That must be our testimony also as leaders. And that was one thing about David—he worked on things until he became skillful.

And the fourth thing is that *he led them.* In other words, he is not sitting in an ivory tower and just issuing commands but he was always walking in the front. David only stopped going into battles when he became a middle aged man and his generals said we want you to be around for a long time so please, you don't have to come to battle with us anymore. We will do the battle you just stay in the palace. Until then he will always walk in the front, always identifying with the people. And you know, have you noticed that the best leaders are leaders who identify with the people? A title does not make a person a leader. The leader should be something that you grow into. And when you identify with people, people see that this is a man who is willing to be one among us. That is the best leader. And for such a leader people will be willing to lay down their lives. And that is why we love our Lord Jesus so much. Because he had all the glory up in heaven. Philippians 2 tells us that he did not consider it to be a robbery to be equal with God. And giving up equality with God to create equality with me? Think about that. Giving up equality with God to create equality with man. That is what Jesus did. How can we not love him?

David was a growing leader. Dr. Elmer Towns presents David as a perfect example of a growing leader. There is something called the Peter principle in leadership. And which states like this, 'employees within an organization will advance to their highest level of competence and then be promoted to and remain at a level at which they are incompetent.' In other words, you begin in an organization at entry level and people begin to see that you are capable you are good and they will promote you to the next level. You do good there and you get promoted to the third level and you go higher up the ladder and then because of all this history there will come a day in your life they will promote you to a level for which you are not ready. That is the Peter principle. And you get stuck at that position and now you had a glorious career coming up along beautifully and then all of a sudden you come up to the next level and you realize that, oh my God, I cannot function at this level. Until now I was doing fine because you got to the limit of your personality.

One reason why it happens is that people stop growing. So if you want to keep advancing you have to keep growing. There is no way around it you have to keep growing. That is why companies invest money into continuous education and tell you to go back to school and take the courses. If you want a promotion take these courses. Why, because if you don't grow to the next level there is no point in promoting you to the next level.

We have two rich sources to help us understand David's growth towards greatness. First is a historical account of his life which is given to us in 1 Samuel, 2 Samuel, 1 Kings & 1 Chronicles. The second source is Psalms that were written by David himself. The Psalms portray the emotional side to David's life. So you can look at the historical side which was written by other people. And you can look at the Psalms which shows the emotional side to this leader which was written by him so we can come to a picture about what kind of a man he was.

Look at both phases of David as a leader. We know that David came to the forefront on the day he killed Goliath and David was only a teenager at that time. And God said, you're going to be the next king in Israel. But the next day he did not become the king.

Let us look at the phases he actually had to go before he became the king.

The first phase was in 1 Samuel 16 when he was serving in the palace. King Saul had an issue where an evil spirit would come upon him and they were looking for someone who was interested in worship. And they wanted a worship leader to come. The only thing that quieted down the spirit of King Saul in those days was someone worshiping God with an instrument. They were looking for somebody and David was brought in. His first experience was as a worship leader. He was brought into the palace and he would take the harp and play and the evil spirit would leave King Saul. That was the first phase.

Then, when we come to 1 Samuel 18 and the second part of verse 5, for the first time king Saul entrusted him with some military responsibilities and he put him over his soldiers because he could see that he has a military leadership gift. The Bible tells us that wherever Saul would send him he would do things with exceeding wisdom. This was the second level of David's leadership development.

The third level of training was at an administration level. He was an administrator under king Saul. In 1 Sam. 18 and the first part of verse 5 we read, "So David went out wherever Saul sent him, and behaved wisely". He was taking care of things for King Saul. He had no problem becoming a second lieutenant. He did not say, hey, God said I'm going to be the next king, the throne is mine. No, none of those issues.

Have you noticed how God is taking him forward? God took him from walking behind the ewes, using his natural talent as a worshipper and an instrumentalist. Our natural gift always comes through in our leadership development and he got an entrance into the king's palace because of that natural gift. And then the king saw what happened to him one day when he defeated Goliath and he realized David is a military genius. So even though he was a young man in his early twenties, he became a military commander. He did such a good job the king began to give him more responsibilities.

Going higher up on the leadership ladder means only one thing—more responsibility. And sometimes it doe snot even bring more money. If you do not want the responsibility, do not expect to go up the ladder. And I know some people have an attitude problem. They say, 'if I stay here for five more minutes I must be paid for that.' That is the attitude of an hourly worker on the floor. If you want to be a leader, more is expected from you. You may have to go in early and leave late. Some people say, 'What do they think I am? I am a fool? Expecting me to show up at 7:00 and my shift starts at 8:00? They think I am a fool to work for them for free for one hour?' Guess what? You are going to stay at the current level, with your attitude, all your life. Then ten or fifteen years later you get very upset you say, 'This is discrimination. I am working here for fifteen years and they never gave me a chance. They never promoted me.' And then you find all kinds of excuses for it. No it's your attitude. You refuse to give even five more minutes for the company. Why should they promote you?

Another interesting thing noted is so close to what happens in your workplace. On one side Saul is giving him more responsibility but on the other side he is trying to sack David. On one side you can see that king Saul is giving him more responsibility because David is doing things good and handling things with wisdom. So his is promoting him. And on the other side after all of that he will go to his family and start cussing at Jonathan and say, 'look at what I had to do for David. I had to promote him. Not because I really want to, but you are no good for anything. I have no choice but to give all this to David.' On one side promoting him and on the other side, trying to sack him.

Isn't it similar to what is happening in many corporations these days? They send you overseas telling you that they are starting an office overseas and they need you to train some people there. But when you return, you realize you were training people to take your job! But when you are going forward in an organization, you have no choice but to assume that responsibility.

The fourth level is found in 1 Samuel 23. David has become a militia leader and there is about 600 people under him. For a while David struggled to find ways to feed them and to protect them. We know the people who joined with David had nothing. So naturally it fell on the shoulders of David to find provisions for them. We have covered some of the incidents during that struggling days in david's life.

After the death of Saul, he became a king in Hebron in 2 Samuel 2. That means he had only two tribes with him at that time, out of the twelve. Only when we come to 2 Samuel 5, finally he became the king over all of the twelve tribes. But it took many years.

He was anointed as a king when he was a teenager but he did not become a king until he was thirty. For many years he just did what the king asked him to do. If you are called for something, God will eventually give you the position. But God will test you to see if you are faithful in little things. And have you noticed that in many of the corporations, the person who become CEO is somebody who started at some lower level and somebody who worked for the company for 40 to 50 years? People get to know them only when they become the CEO and all of a sudden their picture comes in the newspaper and the magazines. But nobody sees them when they are toiling in the back rooms or in the mail rooms doing all the little stuff when you are the water boy and all this stuff. But let me tell you, when you are faithful in little things. Even an earthly organization will reward you one day.

How much more God will honor you? Being a leader is a growth process.

The third aspect about leadership I want to emphasize is something called visionary leadership. Visionary leadership is very important when you want to go somewhere in your life. A visionary is a man who sees things others do not and dare to dreams big. A visionary leader is someone who can make it happen.

All of us have dreams. But very few of you will see it happen. Because you can have dreams and visions but you have to put up the work to see it happen. So that is very important. A visionary sees things that are not there. In today's world you just need one good idea to succeed. But you have to have that idea and then you have to invest everything that you have to see that idea come through. And when people give total dedication for that and they work hard, we see it pays off. How many people have become billionaires in our generation? Michael Dell, Bill Gates of Microsoft, Steve Jobs of Apple are all people who had a dream to do something that was not there. They envisioned a new product in their mind and when people doubted them, they took it as a challenge. And with a single minded dedication, they invested everything they had into that. Look at the worldwide recognition it has brought them. Every student in an MBA program is studying everything about them—about their life, about their commitment and about their leadership. You can be that person. You can be the next Michael Dell. Who says you cannot be the next Bill Gates? You have to have a unique dream. Then you have to pursue it until it comes true.

There are four core elements of spiritual visionary leadership.

1. You have to develop core spiritual values.
2. You have to have a clear vision of what you want to do with your life. f you have to scratch your head, that is not a clear vision.
3. You have to have empowering relationships.
4. You have to take courageous action.

Look at David's visionary leadership. Despite his military success, he was primarily a worshipper and as a result his dream was about the temple of God. When God said you are not the person who is selected to build this temple, he did not stop dreaming about the temple. We can see that he started gathering up resources for that temple. Every time he would go into a battle and he will win a battle, he would take the plunder and he will keep it aside for the temple. And then we can see that towards the end of his life he started inspiring people. He said, 'this is all the things I did for the temple and we want to build the most beautiful temple on the face of the earth so I want you to join with me and give just like I gave' and people started giving. Because he set an example. He was a person who led them.

Dreaming is not enough. You have to see it through. God said, you are not the person who will be building the temple. So he called Solomon and gave him everything. We know Solomon was the wisest person who ever lived on the face of the earth. But do you know who gave the blueprint for the temple? Solomon did not make the blueprint for the temple. David gave him the blueprint for the temple. He said, 'by the way this is the way I want you to build the temple. I have the blueprint ready already.' Why, because for a long time that is all he thought about. He said God has given me a clear vision of how the temple should look. And Solomon just did the work. But the father did all the vision part of it.

Finally, a good leader cannot be a leader without planning for the future. We know that in David's case that was also associated with the temple. When you have responsibilities you have to spend a lot of time planning. And we know that David not only planned for the temple he got the people on his side just before he died. He called all the people together and made sure they are part of that dream. Then he could peacefully hand everything over to Solomon and then exit from the scene.

How are you handling the leadership responsibility that God has given you? What is your dream about your life? How far do you want to go forward? Do you have any big dreams in your life? Or are you just worried about the day to day life? If you allow your circumstances to dictate where you go, the system is built up in such a way that you will be working to pay your bills all your life. The electricity bill, the gas bill, the mortgage bill, the car bill, the insurance bill etc. Is that all you want with your life? Do you have any big dreams about yourself? Do you have something that you want to accomplish for God or for you, something that will make your life meaningful? Hold onto the dream that God has given to you and work for it and pursue it. It may take a while but it will come through. And God will use you and bring glory to his name through your life.

CHAPTER XIX

Passing the Torch

L et us focus on 1 Chronicles 29:36-40 for this study.

"Thus David the son of Jesse ruled over all Israel, the period that he reigned over Israel was over forty years. For seven years he reigned in Hebron and thirty three years he reigned in Jerusalem. So he died in a good old age with riches and honor and Solomon his son reigned in his place. Now the acts of King David the first and the last indeed they are written in the book of Samuel; the seer in the book of Nathan the prophet; and in the book of Gath the seer with all his reign and his might and with all the events that happened to him and to all the kingdom of the lands".

When you read through 1 chronicles you will see that the last two chapters of that book are actually David saying goodbye to his people. We have followed David along from his childhood and we have seen various stages in his life and different experiences that he went through. We saw that he went through a lot of good and bad experiences, up times and down times in his life and we saw that in the midst of all of it there was one thing that stood out about this man—he never questioned his God. Never asked God, why are you putting me through this?

When a person who has gone through so many experiences comes to the end of his life and calls all the leaders of Israel and gives them a review of his life you would expect that he would say some of the bad things that happened in his life. He would probably tell them about some of the toughest times in his life. He would probably try to give them lessons on how he survived those tough times. But what really strikes us is this: When you start reading from chapter 28, he never mentions any of those negative personal experiences. It is really a lesson for all of us. Because most of us are so self absorbed that we are always worried about ourselves and we are covered with self pity. We want everyone to know all the bad things that happen to us. Many times we have this tendency to focus on the negative.

We always say, 'I can't forget this person did this to me. That person did that to me.' David also did mention that in private to Solomon but when he called all the people, if you look at the review process, basically what he talked about was how God led him with his plans. He tells us in chapter 28 and verse 2, he starts sating "as for me". Basically what he is saying is that I had a lot of plans when I was called into leadership and when I was called on the throne. I expected to do certain things for God. But then God came down and changed all those plans. He spent most of the time talking about how God altered his plans.

It is so surprising that a man who went through so much in his life did not talk about his experiences. He only talked about the temple. So that became a lesson for me. When you come to the end of your life and when you look back in the rear view mirror and see the path that you covered or the trail that you blazed, what will be the most important thing you will remember? What will be the thing that sticks out in your mind? And we know that all of us have to say goodbye one day. Hopefully we will get many more years but nonetheless it is inevitable. One thing is for sure: if you are born into this world one day you have to die.

What will stick out in your mind at the end of your life? Is it the bitterness of the betrayal that you had to suffer at the hand of others? Is it people giving up on you? People trying to poison your reputation and your life through gossip?

How many of us will actually focus on God at that time? And tell others, 'Listen, the sum total of my life is this, I wanted to do certain things but God said no. God came down and changed me and said don't do what you want to do, I want you to do what I want you to do.'

How many of us can say that? Take a moment to think about it. What if God asks of an account of our life? Remember what he did with Belshazzar? God declared, 'I measured you. I measured you in a balance and I have found you wanting.' Belshazzar was all about himself. He was very self absorbed despite the spiritual heritage that came into the life of his grandfather, Nebuchadnezzar. If God puts you on a balance now and asks you for an account of your life and if God says, 'you are about to meet Me, get ready to meet your creator', how will you respond?

Let us say He gives us a chance like He gave to Hezekiah. He spoke to King Hezekiah through His prophet and said, 'I'm going to call you to Me, so get your house in order.' It gives you a little bit of time. We know our priorities will change. Oh, how soon our priorities will change! So many things that we think are important will become not important at all.

A few months ago I ended up in the hospital quite unexpectedly and the doctor said I have something wrong with my heart and they had to put three stents in me. The next morning my life had a completely different meaning. Until then I used to tell everyone, 'I am a young man.' But the next morning when I got up I could see the finish line! So all of a sudden it dawns on you that you only have a certain amount of time on the face of this earth. Thank God he has given me a few more years. What am I going to do with that? You prioritize and re-prioritize your life. You get rid of all the silly stuff and you don't pay attention to it. You hear people talking about you but you don't pay any attention because you know you have more serious business to do here. There are plans I want to see accomplished, I have dreams I want to see fulfilled.

So how many of us can actually say, 'Lord, when I come into your presence, what sticks out in my life will not be my wife, not my children, not my struggles in my life, not the days I had no money, not the days I did not sleep and not the days I was crying myself to sleep, not the days when people gave up on me, but with the life you gave me I did what you wanted me to do?'

We see that in the case of David, God came down and forcibly changed his plans. When he became the King his greatest desire was to build a temple in Jerusalem. But God said, 'I did not create you to build a temple. I created you to expand the borders of this land. I created you as a man of war. Don't be ashamed to go into battles because that is what I created you for. Go into the battles, expand the boundaries of this land and in that process you will bring glory to My name.' David did the same.

But he did not fully give up on his dream. He started thinking, 'if God will not let me build the temple, what is the next best thing I can do for that project?' We know that he would put aside all the plunder he got from the conquests and not take it for him. We know that he was struggling for money at that time. Yet he would still put all the plunder aside for the temple. In 1 Chronicles, chapter 28, there is a detailed list about it.

What will you do if God comes and changes up your plans? What will you do if your ambition is shattered? And what will you do when God comes and twists your hand and says, 'I know you are good at this. I know that this is the plan that you have made for yourself. I know you are dedicating so many hours for this. I know you are dreaming about this. I know your computer is full of stuff related to what you want to do. But I did not create you for this so I am changing your life.' Will you allow God to do that? And we know so many people who wanted to go in one direction but God interfered with their life and said no. So don't get frustrated.

I fall into that same category. I never wanted to be a pastor. I had other plans for my life. I just wanted to be a professional and live a quiet life. But God said, 'I am not letting to follow your plans. I created you for a purpose and you may not like it but nonetheless I am still going to interfere with your life.' When push comes to shove He is God. And you can play with Him for a while but there comes a point when God says go and you will go.

Remember the day when God came down into the life of Moses and started beckoning him to 'come'? It's very interesting to study that passage. The first thing God told Moses was 'come.' God was offering a partnership to him and said, 'I will come with you. I will go with you into Egypt. And I will help you accomplish what I want to accomplish for my people.' And Moses would come with excuse and after excuse like 'I cannot speak well', 'Nobody is going to listen to me', 'I have run away from Egypt, how can I go back and face the King?' 'They will put me in jail.' Finally God got angry. It came to a point where Moses was becoming bolder and bolder. When you keep bringing excuses against your call on your life you will get bolder. Because you think that I got away with my past excuses maybe I can get away with this one too. The same thing happened to Moses. He got bolder and bolder and came to a point where he point blank told God to send someone else. "I do not want you to use me, leave me alone. Call somebody else, send somebody else." God just tightened the grip and said, "No! You go." And Moses went. The end of story.

So you have a choice while God is lenient towards you. While he is covering you with grace and saying, 'Come with me, I have plans to use you. I know the thoughts I have for you. It is not thoughts of destruction but thoughts of prosperity. I want to take you somewhere if you are willing to come along with me.' We in foolishness keep resisting until He tightens the grip. And then all of a sudden everything that we were building begins to collapse and then we are ready to listen to God. Do not be found in that spot because I know some of you have God's call upon your life and I know you have been running from God hoping that you can outrun God. You cannot. He will get you because His presence covers this whole universe. You cannot outrun Him.

God did the same with David. God said it would be his son who would build the temple. So he had no choice but to hand everything over to Solomon.

When David handed everything over to Solomon, there was no resentment in his voice. He actually blessed Solomon. He told Solomon in chapter 28, verse 20, "be strong and of good courage to do it. Do not fear nor be dismayed for the Lord my God will be with you. He will not leave you nor forsake you until you have finished all the work for the service of the house of the Lord."

This leads to another question. If you want to do something, you are making plans and then God comes and says no, the plans are good but you are not the one who is going to do it. I have somebody else in mind. Why don't you just hand everything over to this person and step away? How many of us will gladly do that. We would say, "No, these are my plans. All my life I worked towards this and all of a sudden I just have to hand it over and this guy has to do nothing? He takes over and does everything? He gets the glory after I did all the work?" We will be very resentful.

But we can see that there is no resentment in the voice of David. He blessed the person, who was doing that project and said, 'May God strengthen you. May God be with you until you complete the project and may the grace of God be with you.' That is why God called David a man after his own heart.

The second thing that note in this chapter is, "the times that went over him" (1 Chronicles 29:30). How do we get to know God closer? How do we get to appreciate God more? It is through the times that go over us. In chapter 28 when he was sharing this project with Solomon, he used the phrase "when the Lord made me understand by his hand upon me." 'I know a lot of stuff, Solomon. You must be wondering how I know God wanted the temple to be built this way. How do I know the heart of God? How do I know how God thinks? How do I know how God is in His dealings? Only because of the times that went over me or the experiences that I went through.'

Do you know who the people who really know God are? They are the people who have gone through different experiences in their lives. Sometimes when God puts us through certain experiences we question God. We question the wisdom of God when we are going through negative experiences in our lives. How come He did not answer our prayers? There are many that believe if I am a child of God I must be living in the biggest house on the land, I must be driving the most expensive car, I must have a ton of money in the bank—but that's not the experience of many saints. How come?

Do you know what David would tell you? 'Just like God's hands were upon me; realize that His hands are upon you. He is sending you through a school; sending you through different experiences.' We can see a beautiful expression of that in Psalm 42:7, even though David did not write that Psalm. It says, "All your waves and billows have gone over me." How many of you have been under a wave lately? How many of you can say, waves are going over my head? Waves and billows; I can feel it; things are coming at me again and again. A psalmist said, 'all your waves and billows have gone over me.'

The funny thing with walking with God is that His hand is upon you. The Bible tells us that He is writing a saga, each of our lives is like a book written on the templates of flesh of our heart. So when God takes the inscribing pen, and puts His heavy hands on your chest and starts writing on the walls of your heart; you will feel it. And when that pressure hits you, it is tough to take.

In Psalm 42, even though the psalmist said all your waves and billows are going over me, he is not complaining. What is the first verse of Psalm 42? 'As the deer pants for the water, my heart pants after you.' On one side I see the waves and I see the billows. On one side I can see the negative incidents, I can feel the heartaches, the pains in my life but nonetheless I am still running to you Lord. I come back to you, I run back into your presence because I know this is your hand upon my life.

How many of us can say when the biggest heartaches happen in our life, it is God's hand on my life? How many can say that when our plans fall apart, it does not matter, it is His hand upon my life, he is writing something new in my life? When your dreams fall apart, how many can say as children of God it is his hand writing something new in your life? It is the beginning of a new chapter in my life so I do not regret and I do not have any resentment. Just as the hymn by Divilla D. Martin says, "His eyes is on the sparrow and I Know he watches me."

How do you measure where you are? Do not look at the situation or the particular issue you are facing. Just look around to see if His hand is still on you. If you are still under the embrace of that everlasting arm you do not have to worry because the Bible declares, 'There is no God like the God of Jeshurun, underneath the everlasting arms! The hands that have gripped you are His everlasting arms! The hands that are embracing you are everlasting arms indeed! No one can pluck you away from there. Be comfortable under that embrace. That is why David said in Psalm 31:15, "My times are in your hand." If it is in His hand, I can leave it there and I know the end result will be fine. If you have any doubt, just look at David, what he went through and where he ended up.

Thirdly, during this time period in his life, he made it clear that he is leaving a spiritual heritage behind. He told his son Solomon in 1 Chronicles 28:9, "As for you my son Solomon, *know the God of your father*". It is a very powerful statement. He did not say know the God of Abraham, Isaac and Jacob. That would have been a general statement. But he said, 'Follow the God your father has followed.' The greatest desire in the heart of every father and mother who is a Christian is to see their children taking the same Bible they took in their hands and standing for the same truth that they stood for. But let me tell you, in order for them to do that, we need to make God our own first. So that at the end of our life, we can look at our sons and daughters and say, 'Follow the God of your father.' We should have such a beautiful relationship with this true and living God.

How is your relationship with your God? Before you start worrying about your children think about yourself. Can you confidently go to your child and say, 'Follow God the way I am following?' That must be our confidence. One of the greatest tragedies in the world today is that many people cannot say that. Yet that is the desire of every Christian parent.

I remember my son coming to me when he was about thirteen and I was just in the early days of my ministry. He asked me, "Dad, do you expect me to become a pastor?" I still remember that conversation. I told him, "No, I don't expect you to become a pastor but if God calls you, you become a pastor." And later on looking at where his life has gone from that day, sometimes I wonder if I gave him the wrong answer. Sometimes I wonder if I had told him, "Yes, I want you to become a pastor when you grow up so make sure you live according to that," he would have been more careful. I know ultimately I gave the right answer because I am not the one who calls somebody to be a pastor, God is the one. If God calls him to be a pastor one day, it would be the greatest joy of my life. I will not have any problem with that but I would never force him to become a pastor. But I have one desire about all three of my children that they should be truthful to Bible because in the prime of my youth, I gave up a lot to follow this and to be a minister. After I sacrificed so much and I lived for many years very sacrificially, when I come to the end of my life if my children are not following God, I would really feel like a failure. Nothing would give me a sense of failure than the children not wanting to do anything with the God I served.

It is very important that David would challenge his son and ask him to know the God of your father. He is saying that your father came to know God through the experiences that he went through and it was a lifetime journey, a lifetime of experiences that made him know who God is and how God works and how to serve God. Submit yourself to follow God for a lifetime the same way. We know that unfortunately, Solomon did not do that. He started out that way but eventually others pulled his heart away from his God. He was not truthful for a lifetime. He was committed for a while. Then he went away from God.

Your parents probably told you, "Son, daughter, know the God of your father. Commit yourself to follow the God of your father." If your father had challenged you but you have been running away from this God, I beckon you to come back to God. There are people who have been running away from their call. It is time for you to go back and look for that old Bible. Take old worn out Bible that your father carried and say, 'From this day forward I will follow the God of my father. I will serve him truthfully as my father served him.' That will be a day of joy in heaven.

There is a second spiritual heritage David left for Solomon. David was a man that gave freely to the work of God. Look at the statement from David in 1 Chronicles 28:14. It must become a standard for us. "In my trouble, I have prepared all this". That means David did not wait until he was wealthy when he started giving to God. He did not say, 'When I have a lot of money I will start giving to God. After my house is paid off, my car is paid off; after I put my children through college I will start honoring God with my finances.' From the early days of his conquests he would take the plunder and keep it aside for the building of the temple in Jerusalem. At that time he had nothing. Remember in one of our studies we saw that a neighboring King had to come and build the palace for David because he had no money to build a palace for himself. Even then, he would put money away for the temple. I want to ask you, how is your giving to God? Do you truthfully give?

Some people have a big issue with tithing. He only asks for ten percent. Ninety percent is yours. Ten is the number of redemption in the Bible. So what God is saying is if you honor me with that ten percent, I will make sure that you get to use the ninety percent. Many times we do not focus on the ninety percent; we only focus on the ten percent. We know that when God says I will redeem the ninety percent, it means that your car will not unnecessarily break down; you will not have many unexpected expenses.

Our family knows from our experiences that the reason for not having enough money is because of the unexpected expenses during a given month. Even is your check bounces because you are short of one cent, the bank takes $35 from you. Many times we make money, but we do not get to use all of it. God said, when you honor me with your tithes, I redeem the rest of the money so that you get to use it, so that there will be more than enough for you. The funny thing is some people will have a tough time writing a hundred dollar check to church in a month but they have no problem paying for four bounced checks during that same month and giving the bank $140 in bank fees! So which way do you want to live? It is your choice.

David said, 'in my trouble, when I had nothing, I started giving.' How do you get out of your poverty? How do you get out of your trouble? By honoring God! It is not just our hard work that brings blessings in our life; it is the favor of God. When you are walking in obedience with God, you automatically begin to receive the favor of God in your life and God begin to open doors for you. You realize that you are walking in the blessings of God. That is why Jesus said, 'Seek ye first the kingdom of God and his righteousness and all these things will be added to you.'

David is not the only person who did that. In 2 Corinthians 8:1, Paul says, "Moreover brethren, we make known to you the grace of God bestowed on the churches of Macedonia." That was a church going through persecution at that time. Look at Paul's testimony about that church: "in a great trial of affliction the abundance of their joy and their deep poverty abounded in the riches of their liberality". Wow, that is a message in itself! This was a church that had learned to give, in the midst of deep poverty. It is an unchangeable principle in this world that if you sow something, you will get a harvest.

The Bible teaches us that if you honor God, God will honor you in return. God is not obligated to anyone. Recently, I was thinking of somebody in our church, of somebody who was so gracious when we were getting ready to buy our church building, someone who gave a tremendous offering for the building project. I used to wonder how he managed to do it because I know that he is not an extremely wealthy man. But this week I saw what God gave him in return for that. On my way back to my house I was thanking God. I could say, God you are a faithful God.

David said, 'in my trouble I started honoring God. When I had nothing I started giving for the work of God and God has blessed me abundantly.' Plus, he tells us what he gave from his own funds.

"Moreover, because I have set my affection on the house of my God, I have given to the house of my God, over and above all that I have prepared for the holy house, my own special treasure of gold and silver: three thousand talents of gold, of the gold of Ophir, and seven thousand talents of refined silver, to overlay the walls of the houses; the gold for [things of] gold and the silver for [things of] silver, and for all kinds of work [to be done] by the hands of craftsmen." (1 Chronicles 29: 3-5).

David is giving generously from his wealth because God blessed him so much. Some of you may not have a lot of money but if you start honoring God in your trouble, when you do not have enough money to meet your monthly expenses, God will honor you. You will not end where you are today. You will see how God is going to honor you.

The third thing about his spiritual heritage is in found in 1 Chronicles, chapter 28, verse 11. "Then David gave his son Solomon the plans for the vestibule, its houses, its treasuries, its upper chambers, its inner chambers and the place of the mercy seat and the plans that all he had by the spirit of the courts of the house of the Lord and all the chambers all around". And then there is a long list of details to follow. In verse 19, David told Solomon, 'all these detailed instructions that I am giving to you, the Lord made me understand in writing by his hand.'

We know that God gave the plan to Moses to build the tabernacle. Now David says, 'I can give you all this detailed information because God gave it to me in writing.' The blueprint for the Jerusalem temple came from God! David, how did you get to the level where you were able to obtain the inner secrets of God's court? It was because of a lifetime of walking with God. God never keeps secrets from his dear friends. The spirit of God begins to reveal things to you. You begin to get visions, you begin to get dreams, you begin to get words of knowledge and when you lay hands on people, sometimes things in their lives begin to show up as if it were on a screen. People begin to wonder and say that guy is just making that up. But let me tell you, it is not a lie, it is not a made up story. It has happened to me many times even though I do not consider myself a prophet. When you begin to walk closer to God, *uninterruptedly*, you begin to get closer to the heart of God and God begins to impart more and more into your life.

Who is David talking to? The wisest man who ever lived on the earth! Who was given the plan? The man who walked with God! So who is on a higher plateau? The wisest man on earth or the man who walks with God?

There is a problem with many of us. We would rather listen to gurus on television than to the Holy Spirit. There is nothing wrong with listening to leadership gurus and others. I have two kids who just graduated with MBAs in my house and when they are out I go and read the stuff they had to read because I love reading. Many times, I can see it is good stuff. I am not negating the impact of those things but it is better to listen to the Holy Spirit! This is very important to remember—a man of God is never at the mercy of a man of the world. Solomon was the wisest guy who ever lived in history but who is giving him the plans? The man who walked with God, the man who could say 'I have received this from God.' David gave Solomon the plans and the money. He just had to carry out the plans.

Finally, when we come to chapter 29, we see David throwing a going away party. This is some way to end one's life journey! I do not think everyone will get this privilege. David knew his time was coming and he threw a great going away party. Look at chapter 29, verses 20 to 22. "And then David said to all assembly, now bless the Lord your God and all the assembly blessed the Lord God of their fathers and bowed their heads and prostrated themselves before Lord and the King".

Let us stop there for a moment. The people who follow God know only one thing—to worship. David put his son on the throne handed the plans to him and handed the gold and silver to him and gave one big party to everyone who was gathered there. But he turned the party into a prayer meeting. See this is the problem with the children of God. Everything is a prayer meeting for them.

One day my children came to me and said, 'we never had a birthday party.' I said, 'What do you mean you never had a birthday party?' We had a birthday party every year for them. They said, 'No, you never had a birthday party, you only had a prayer meeting.' It was so true! I am guilty of that. We turn everything into a prayer meeting. We would have a prayer meeting in our house and we would call the whole church. We would have nice food and we would pray for them and then we cut the cake. That was their birthday party for many years. Only after they became adults did they begin to celebrate their birthdays with their friends.

David did the same thing. "And they made sacrifices to the Lord and made burn offerings to the Lord on the next day a thousand bulls, a thousand rams, a thousand lambs with their drink offerings and sacrifices in abundance for all Israel". The last phrase is very important. So we know that this is not a complete burning up of the flesh of a thousand bulls and a thousand rams and a thousand lambs. It is a type of sacrifice called the 'zebah' which was a thanksgiving sacrifice (Leviticus 7:12). In that sacrifice all they burned on the altar was the intestines and the fat. Then the priest will bless that sacrificial animal and give it back to the person who brought it. Then they can have a party in the name of the Lord. They will celebrate with that meat. When the Bible says that David did a sacrifice enough for all Israel, it does not mean the whole nation but all the people who were gathered there. How many animals did he kill that day? A thousand bulls, a thousand rams and a thousand lambs and enough drink offering to go with that. What a huge party! And everyone rejoiced.

Then David put his son Solomon on the throne and handed everything over to him. This is very important. A leader's job is not finished until he or she develops a successor. We know that many organizations fail, many churches fail because they have no successors. A true leader knows that while he is alive and well he has to develop successors.

Remember how Saul left the scene? He left the nation in a mess. But David being a man of God did things according to what God taught him. He learned how to follow God and did things properly. He organized everything, did everything properly, put the successor on the throne and gave a party to everyone and stepped down and within a short time he was gone. In verse 28, we read that David "died in a good old age full of days and riches and honor."

When you commit yourself to serve God at a young age, this is the way you can end your life. This should be the last statement about your life. You got to live a good life. You went through experiences but you learned from all those experiences and God turned all of them into blessings into your life. Despite all the early struggles, when you come to the end of your life you can go back and say this was worth it. Look at the way I am exiting from the world with honor and riches and everything in order! Not leaving a mess behind. You can go peacefully into eternity and meet your creator—a glorious end to a glorious life.

In conclusion, this is what I want to ask you. Someone has said, "Only one life to live, and it will soon pass, only the things done for the Lord will last." What kind of a life do you want to live? Some of you are young. You are just starting out in your life. You have a whole life ahead of you. Decide today, how you are going to live? Some of us, like me, have reached the middle age so we cannot do anything about the years that are already gone. We can make plans to redeem the rest of the time that is given to us on the face of the earth and make some changes. You can make plans and reprioritize your life so that others will say at the end of your life that you lived a meaningful life. He lived a life of honor. He left things behind in an orderly fashion and he has died with riches and honor. Yes, you can do that.

That is why the Bible says today is the day of salvation. This is a grace period in your life. God is giving you another opportunity to reorganize your life. If your life is in a mess in any area, it does not have to be that way for one more day. God is ready to give you another chance. He will put things in order. All you have to do is to submit yourself to follow his plans for your life and things will begin to change. Things will all fall into place. Can you commit yourself into the hand of God?

Short Biography of the Author

Dr. Sunny Philip has been in ministry since 1986 as a Pastor, Conference Speaker, Denominational Leader and Revivalist. Currently he serves as the Senior Pastor of Gateway World Christian Center in Long Island, New York, which is a multicultural, full gospel fellowship. Under his leadership the Global Network of Christian Indian Leaders was formed in 2004.

Dr. Philip is renowned in many parts of the world for rightly dividing the word. He has ministered in many African nations, many Asian nations, Australia, Europe and across North and Central Americas. He regularly writes in periodicals and has published four books. His teaching CDs and DVDs are available at www.gatewaynyc.com and www.sphilipministries.com.

Sorry about the mistakes we did not
catch before the printing. It was partly
because of rushing the print to make
copies available for the conference.
Revisions are underway.

9 781463 416492